SEEKING THE NORTHWEST PASSAGE

The Explorations and Discoveries of Champlain and Hudson

Don and Carol Thompson

Donald H. Thompson

Carol L. Thompson

PURPLE MOUNTAIN PRESS

Fleischmanns, New York

First Edition 2008

Published by Purple Mountain Press, Ltd.
P.O. Box 309, Fleischmanns, New York 12430-0309
845-254-4062, 845-254-4476 (fax), purple@catskill.net
http://www.catskill.net/purple

ISBN-13: 978-1-930098-90-9
ISBN: 1-930098-88-90-1
Library of Congress Control Number: 2008932986

Cover: *The Half Moon*, painting copyright © 2003
by L. F. Tantillo (lftantillo.com)

Illustration credit
Pages 15, 47, 48, and 71: drawings by Andrew Thompson.
Page 16: photo by permission of Kevin Shields.
Page 28: from the collection of Russell Bellico.
Page 77: photo by Russell Bellico.
Maps and all other photos are by Donald Thompson.
Other illustrations are from the authors' collection

Manufactured in the United States of America on acid-free paper.

5 4 3 2 1

Contents

Champlain's 1632 Map of North America   4

Introduction   5

Chapter 1: Early Life and Travels   7

Chapter 2: Champlain Attempts to Establish
New France, 1604-1608   13

Chapter 3: Henry Hudson's Attempts to Find a
Shortcut to Asia   20

Chapter 4: 1609, An Eventful Year   27

Chapter 5: Henry Hudson Returns to North America   36

Chapter 6: Hudson Explores the River of Mountains   44

Chapter 7: Champlain Helps his Indian Allies and
Explores the Interior, 1610-1616   52

Chapter 8: Champlain, the Father of New France   61

Chapter 9: Henry Hudson's Final Attempt to Find
a Northwest Passage, 1609-1611   66

Chapter 10: The Legacy of Champlain and Hudson   73

Epilogue: Celebrations, Past and Future   75

Champlain and Hudson Timeline   78

Glossary   80

Bibliography   82

Index   84

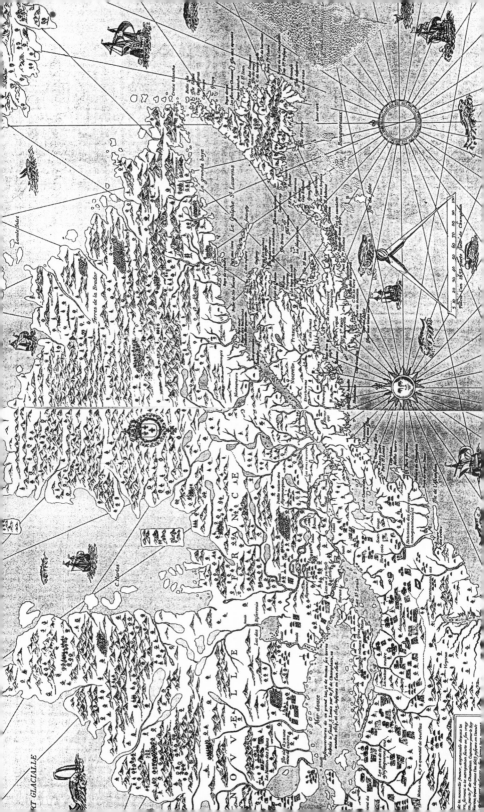

Introduction

Explorers Samuel de Champlain and Henry Hudson lived about the same time and had many things in common. They were born around 1570, although the exact dates are not known. Both were sons of sea captains involved in trade. The two future explorers grew up learning navigational skills from an early age. Eventually each sailed west to search for a northwest passage that would provide a shorter route from Europe to the spice trade in Asia. They both found unexpected natural resources in North America. Both traded successfully with Native Americans, but both also had armed conflict with them. The conflicts often resulted in loss of life.

Portraits of explorers Champlain and Hudson.

These portraits have been copied many times, but no actual portraits exist, so no one knows for sure what they really looked like.

Facing page: **Champlain's 1632 Map of North America**

While they were born around the same time and both explored North America, one important difference is the length of time during which their explorations took place.

Champlain had a much longer career as an explorer and outlived Hudson by about twenty-five years. Hudson's brief career as an explorer lasted only about four years, from 1607-1611. His explorations and life ended abruptly and tragically when his crew mutinied and set him adrift in Hudson Bay in 1611. This book first will give background on what little is known of the two explorers' early lives, and their explorations before 1608. The main focus will be on their journeys during the summer and fall of 1609, when their routes took them into what is now New York State. Samuel de Champlain traveled south on Lake Champlain to help his Indian allies fight their enemies, the Mohawk Iroquois, part of the Haudenosaunee Confederacy. Henry Hudson sailed his *Half Moon* up the River of Mountains (as he called the Hudson) hoping it would lead to the Northwest Passage. Although both men explored present-day New York State in 1609, they never met. However, each had an important role in the history of New York.

Chapter 1
Early Life and Travels

It is believed that Samuel de Champlain and Henry Hudson were born some time between 1565-1570. Exact records were not kept in those days, so their actual birth dates are unknown. During this late Renaissance period, the countries of western Europe were developing art, music, science, and trade. They were especially interested in the valuable spice trade with Asia. Spices such as cinnamon, ginger and cloves were in demand for flavoring and to disguise the taste of food that wasn't fresh, in the days when refrigeration was not yet available. The spice trade was controlled by Italian city-states like Venice and Genoa. When these city states began fighting, some explorers left to sail for other countries. Giovanni Caboto (John Cabot) went to England, and Giovanni da Verrazano left Florence to sail for France. Verrazano became the first European known to have sailed into the mouth of the Hudson River. As word came back after exploration, European countries started to realize they had found a new continent with its own rich resources of codfish, beaver furs, and possibly gold. During this time of European exploration, Samuel de Champlain and Henry Hudson were growing up in port cities, Champlain in France and Hudson in England.

Champlain's Early Life

Samuel de Champlain was born to Antoine de Complain and Margueritte LeRoy in Brouage, on the Bay of Biscay. Brouage was a fishing and salt-making center. The salt was produced by evaporating sea water. It was used to preserve fish. French fishing boats headed to the Grand Banks off Newfoundland would take on salt at Brouage to keep their catch of codfish from spoiling.

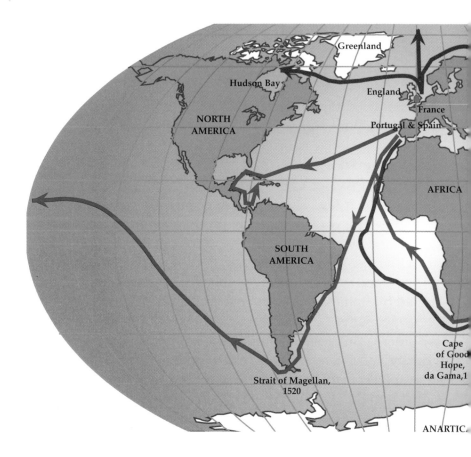

Brouage also was a center for French Protestants called Huguenots. It is possible that young Samuel grew up as a Protestant and became a Catholic as an adult. Samuel went to sea with his father on the fishing boats and learned the skills of navigation and mapmaking. He also was skilled at drawing, a talent he would use later as he explored North America.

As a child, Samuel witnessed religious wars fought over control of France. During the 1590s, while in his twenties, he was a quartermaster in the royal army. He was paid 75 *livres*, about $15 a month. In 1594 he was part of an English and French attack on Fort Crozat that was attempting to drive out Spanish invaders. By chance he served under Sir

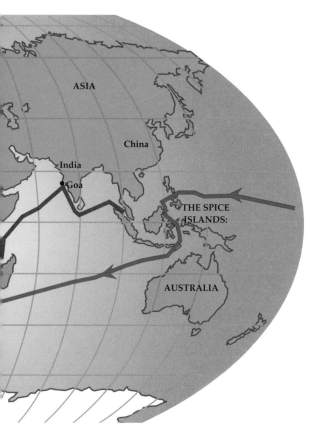

Early European
Voyages of Discovery

Blue:
The route of Vasco
da Gama of Portugal,
1499.

Red:
The Route of
Ferdinand Magellan
of Portugal, 1519-
1522. He died before
his ship returned to
Europe.

Purple:
Champlain's first
voyage to the New
World in 1599.

Brown:
Hudson's search for a
northern passage to
the Spice Islands.

Martin Frobisher, a famous English explorer who had searched for the Northwest Passage. Frobisher lost his life in the battle. When the war was over four years later, Samuel's Uncle Guillaume Hellaine invited Samuel to go on his ship, the *Saint Julian*, when it took captured Spanish troops back to their homeland.

After a few months in Spain, the *Saint Julian* became part of the annual fleet that brought supplies to the Spanish in the Americas and returned loaded with Aztec and Inca gold. Champlain traveled in Spanish-held territory for two and a half years, visiting Puerto Rico, the Virgin Islands, Cuba, the Isthmus of Panama, and Mexico City. Everywhere he went he took notes and made illustrations. He returned

9

Champlain's illustration of gum extraction from a locust tree from his 1602 book on the Spanish West Indies, *Brief Discours*.

to France in 1601 and published a book about his West Indies voyages entitled *A Brief Discours*. It contained detailed drawings of the native people, fruits and animals he had observed.

When he returned to France in 1601, Champlain received a yearly royal pension from King Henry IV and a title of nobility. While at court, he met the man in charge of the fur trade in what is now Canada and was asked to join an expedition in 1603. The fleet left Honfleur, France, on March 15, 1603. They sailed through storms, fog, and a mass of ice, but finally made it up the Gulf of St. Lawrence to the fur-trading center of Tadoussac. They arrived just as the Algonquin and Montagnais Indians were having a great feast to celebrate victory over their enemies, the Iroquois. Champlain recorded in his next book, *Des Sauvages* (*The Savages*), that the feast included "moose, venison, beaver meat and seal blubber all boiled together in great kettles." Champlain did not seem to mind the food but was shocked at his hosts' table manners, especially their habit of wiping their greasy hands in their own hair or on their dogs. The French wanted to trade for furs and also to learn more about finding a Northwest Passage, so they pledged to support the Algonquins and Montagnais against the Iroquois.

On June 18, 1603, Champlain sailed up the St. Lawrence River to a spot called Kebec (Quebec), an Indian word meaning "narrowing of waters." On this site in 1535, French explorer Jacques Cartier's sailors had built a fort. Champlain chose Quebec for the site of a trading post and future colony because of its rich soil and abundant fishing. It was also easily defensible. From his Indian allies he heard of a waterway that stretched westward through large lakes, and thought it might be a passageway to Asia.

In mid-September 1603, the French fleet returned to France with enough fur pelts and dried fish to pay for almost half the original cost of the voyage. The next year, 1604, the fleet was commanded by Pierre du Gua, sieur (Sir) de Monts. De Monts chose a site for settlement in Acadia, which included the area of present-day Nova Scotia, New Brunswick, and northeastern Maine. Champlain had recommended Quebec.

Hudson's Early Life

Little is known about Henry Hudson's childhood and early life. He is thought to have been born some time around 1570 in Hoddersdon, England, north of London. His grandfather, also named Henry Hudson, was a navigator and was involved with the creation of the Muscovy Company. This company was started in 1555 to trade with Russia. It is likely that young Henry's career as an explorer and captain began as a cabin boy and later as an apprentice with the Muscovy Company, where he learned navigational skills.

Before the end of the 1400s, Portuguese explorers were sailing around the Cape of Good Hope at the southern tip of Africa. Vasco da Gama was the first European to sail all the way to India in 1498. From these explorations the Portuguese developed a monopoly of the spice trade coming from India, China, and the Spice Islands (present-day Indonesia). Well-to-do Europeans wanted spices like pepper, cinnamon, cardamom, cloves, and ginger to season their food. They also wanted silk, chinaware, and gold from

Asia. The Spanish controlled the riches coming from the Americas, thanks to the early explorations of Christopher Columbus. By 1602, the Dutch East India Company was formed in the Netherlands to trade with Asia, challenging Portugal's control of the spice trade.

Examples of spices from China and the Spice Islands. Left to right: cardamom seed, nutmeg and mace, peppercorns, ginger root, cinnamon sticks, cloves, and star anise.

Some historians believe that as early as 1587, the teenage Henry Hudson was first mate under English Captain John Davis, who was making his third attempt at finding the Northwest Passage. If Davis had been successful in finding a quicker route to Asia, England would have been the winner in the race to be the wealthiest nation. A story is told that Hudson took over at the wheel and steered the ship all night when Davis was knocked unconscious during a storm. In the morning Davis decided not to continue, as it was becoming too late in the season. No proof of that story exists, but if Hudson had been on that trip, it may explain his later determination to find the Northwest Passage.

Nothing more is known of Hudson's life for the next twenty years until the Muscovy Company hired him to be captain of the *Hopewell* in 1607. By that time he had a wife, Katherine, and three sons: Oliver, John, and Richard. They lived in a three-story brick house not far from the Tower of London.

Chapter 2
Champlain Attempts to Establish New France
1604-1608

The King of France granted wealthy Sieur de Monts and other investors a ten-year fur-trading monopoly in 1604. The land grant stretched from present-day Philadelphia to Newfoundland. In return the investors agreed to send 100 settlers to North America to establish a settlement in New France. Once arriving in North America, Samuel de Champlain was given command of a small ship and crew of eleven men to locate a suitable spot for the settlement along the coast. After looking along the Nova Scotia coastline they crossed the Bay of Fundy and chose an island in the Sainte Croix River. This site was near the border of what is now Maine and New Brunswick. They named the island Sainte-Croix, or "Holy Cross." The island was chosen for its good defense against surprise attacks by the Indians or the English.

In mid-June Champlain's group of 80 men built a small village from precut wood brought from France. Except for annoying swarms of black flies and mosquitoes, summer on Sainte-Croix was not too bad, but with the arrival of winter, life became difficult.

During the fall of 1604 Champlain made two explorations by boat. One took him up the Bay of Fundy to look for possible copper deposits. The other voyage went down the Atlantic coast to search for a rumored city of gold, Norumbega. They sailed past what is today Acadia National Park and around many small islands in Penobscot Bay, mapping and taking depth measurements as they went. Near the end of September the weather became stormy, and Champlain and his crew returned to Sainte-Croix to face the winter.

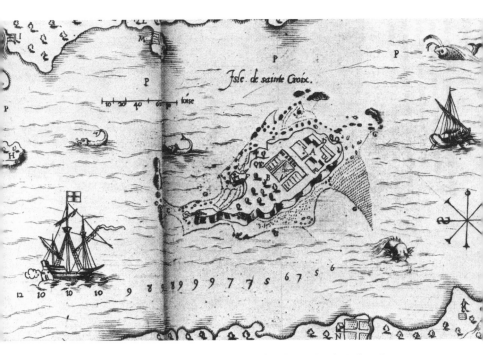

**Champlain's drawing of Sainte-Croix Island
from his 1613 *Les Voyages*.**

By winter the island's fresh water spring dried up, and drinking water couldn't be taken from the salty river. All firewood had to be brought from the mainland because the island didn't have enough trees. Winter arrived early in 1604, with snow on October 6. By December the settlement was cut off from its water and firewood supply by ice floes.

Scurvy, a disease caused by a lack of vitamin C in the diet, took 35 lives that winter, and many more were very ill. Champlain had heard there was a native tree that had helped Cartier's expedition in 1535-36, but he did not know how to identify it. The Indians had taught Cartier how to make a tea from white cedar or northern white pine bark, which would prevent and cure scurvy. Without this knowledge, Champlain's group suffered greatly. Scurvy causes bleeding under the skin, pain in the joints, bleeding gums, loss of teeth, and finally death.

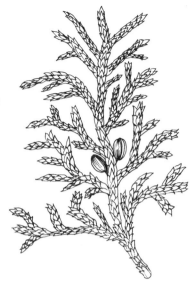

White cedar, the Indian cure for scurvy.

Champlain recorded in *Les Voyages* that scurvy was brought under control in March when they were able to trade with the Indians for some freshly killed game.

By mid-May 1605, Sieur de Monts was ready to abandon Sainte-Croix. One effect of the scurvy outbreak was that the King of France refused to finance any further colonization between 1609-1612. Once it was understood that this disease was caused by a lack of fresh fruits and vegetables or lightly cooked fresh meat in the diet, scurvy was no longer a threat to the survival of New France.

The survivors of the winter at Sainte-Croix were in desperate shape until a supply ship arrived from France in June 1605. Sieur de Monts and Champlain departed on an exploratory voyage down the New England coast to find a better place to settle. Along the coast of Maine they found friendly Indians whom Champlain sketched tending their corn hills, pole beans, pumpkins, and tobacco.

The coastline of Maine at Acadia National Park.

In July 1605, the French sailed into Boston Bay and the bay that would become Plymouth Harbor. They met large numbers of Aptucxet Indians there. These native people would all be wiped out by diseases brought by Europeans before the Pilgrims arrived in 1620.

The expedition continued along the shoreline of Cape Cod and stopped to collect spring water in large kettles. Some nearby Nauset Indians seized one of the kettles, which started a battle with the French sailors. Champlain recorded in his log that he thought the natives were "great thieves." The voyage along the coast ended without finding a good place for a permanent settlement.

When they returned to Sainte-Croix, Sieur de Monts rejected Champlain's suggestions of Penobscot Bay or the St. John River. He chose instead the site of Port Royal on the Nova Scotia coast for the new settlement. All the buildings at Sainte-Croix were taken down and brought across the Bay of Fundy to be rebuilt into a fort-like square, called a *habitation*.

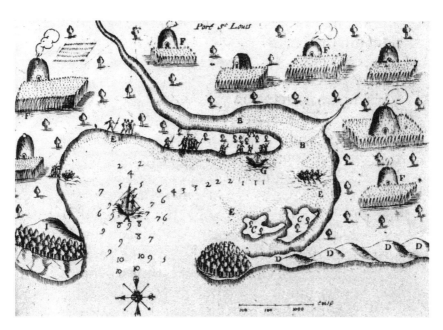

Above: Champlain's 1613 chart of Port Saint-Louis, later called Plymouth Colony, from *Les Voyages. Below:* Port Royal Habitation replica, based on Champlain's 1613 drawing in *Les Voyages.*

The winter of 1605-06 was not as harsh as the previous winter, although scurvy claimed the lives of 12 out of the 45 people living at the Habitation. When spring came, Champlain made a third voyage down the coast of New England. He wanted to sail directly to Cape Cod, but his commander wished to see the coast of Maine first, taking valuable time. The voyage was further delayed by a series of misfortunes. While baking bread on the beach near Chatham, five Frenchmen were killed by Indians. The French tried to get revenge, but lost several more men. Champlain's third voyage ended just a few miles south of where he had been the year before. They returned to Port Royal in mid-November. This was Champlain's last exploration of the Atlantic coast, a major disappointment to a navigator who, had they continued south, might have claimed present-day New York harbor before the Dutch and English.

Champlain might have considered the two years spent at Port Royal his most memorable and enjoyable. He formed the Order of Good Cheer, a social group, and made himself its first grand master. Local Indians were invited to a feast, and each time a different member of the Order would be responsible for bartering with them for moose, caribou, or duck. This friendly trade provided an abundance of food such as beaver tail, wildcat, sturgeon, goose and venison. The French baked fresh bread daily.

A garden was planted near the Habitation, and a spring-fed pond supplied fresh trout. A reservoir at the harbor held sea perch and rock codfish. Besides enjoying this large variety of food, the French put on entertainment to help pass the long winter. They sang songs or invented new ones on the spot. The first play ever presented in Canada, *Neptune*, featuring "tritons" (sea people) and "savages," was staged at Port Royal.

On May 24, 1607, bad news reached Port Royal. Sieur de Monts had lost his trade monopoly because of pressure on the King by rival fur traders. Champlain and most of the others left Port Royal, with only eight or nine men remaining. After 1607 Champlain would never again see Acadia and Port Royal, but he had made his mark. To this day his charts illustrate the accuracy of his depth soundings, and many of his place names still exist. In 1608 Champlain established a permanent trading post at Quebec to avoid competition along the coast, opening up a vast source of animal pelts. He also still hoped to find a possible water route to the riches of Asia.

Champlain's three voyages down the coast of Acadia and New England, 1604-1606

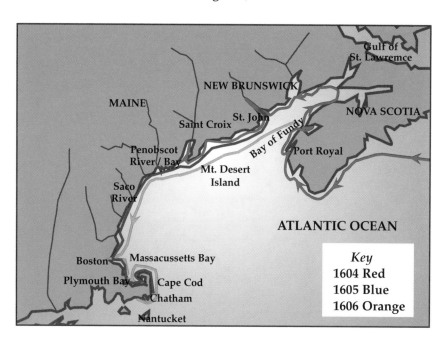

Chapter 3
Henry Hudson's Attempts to Find a Shortcut to Asia

By 1607 England, Holland, France, and Russia all had the goal to find a Northeast passage, a shortcut to Asia. Robert Thorne, a merchant interested in promoting trade, and Richard Hakluyt, a well-known geographer, recommended Hudson take the ship *Hopewell* straight over the North Pole. Thorne and Hakluyt believed that in the sum-

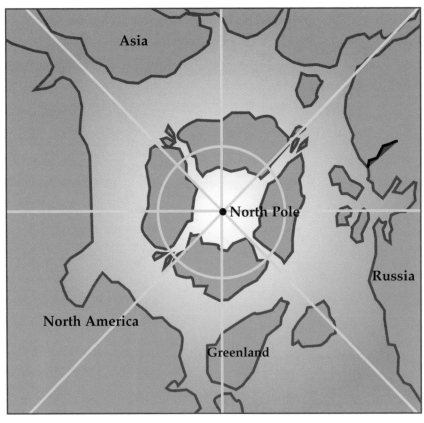

**Polar projection map after Mercator's 1569 *Atlas*.
Mercator's map encouraged explorers to attempt to sail over
the North Pole because it showed open water.**

mer, when the sun shines continuously on the North Pole, the ice would be thin enough for ships to break through.

Mapmakers of Hudson's time showed a northern open water passage to Asia that would be shorter than sailing south around Africa or South America. The Mercator Polar Projection Map of 1569 shows open water beyond Nova Zembla, or "New Land." It was believed that once past the Ob River, the temperature would be warmer for the rest of the voyage to Asia.

When Katherine Hudson learned her husband had agreed to undertake such a long and dangerous journey for a salary of 100 pounds (about $3,000), she was furious. She insisted he ask the Muscovy Company for more money. After all, he was risking his own life and that of their teenage son, John, who was sailing with his father as a cabin boy. The embarrassed Hudson went back to the directors, and after much discussion, they increased his pay by 30 pounds in view of his experience.

Food for a long voyage: dried peas, oatmeal, and salted codfish.

The *Hopewell* was three years old, weighed eighty tons, and already had made six major voyages. In preparation for the trip the *Hopewell's* seams were freshly caulked. Supplies, including dried beef, pickled beef and pork, dried peas, onions and barley meal, were loaded for the long voyage. They also brought along several barrels of salt to preserve any fish they caught. Hudson hoped a cargo of salted fish would make the voyage more profitable. The ship carried twelve crew members, including First Mate John Colman.

In mid-April 1607, Hudson and his crew attended a special service at the Church of St. Ethelburga in London, one of the few buildings that has survived until today. However, the *Hopewell* could not set sail until May 1, because of bad weather and heavy fog. Instead of heading due north, Hudson steered toward Iceland and mapped the east coast of Greenland. At the start of the voyage it seemed the theories about the warmer temperatures near the Arctic in summer might be true. They did not hit bad storms or heavy ice. By the end of June they had reached the Arctic archipelago of Spitsbergen, with its snowcapped mountain peaks.

On July 14, 1607, John Hudson took depth measurements near the entrance to a large bay, using a leaded line. At first it was 30 fathoms, or 180 feet deep, but the water soon became too deep to measure. The crew spotted many whales in the bay. One got caught in the ship's fishing lines and came under the ship, but fortunately caused no damage. This discovery of whales at Spitsbergen led to the development of a whaling industry there. Eventually whaling ships came to the area from many different countries, and the Dutch established the settlement of Smeerenburg, which means "blubber town." Without intending it, Hudson had found a very valuable resource for the Muscovy Company. Whale oil was used for lighting, perfume, and soap, and the bones were used to stiffen women's corsets. For his discovery of this resource, Hudson apparently got

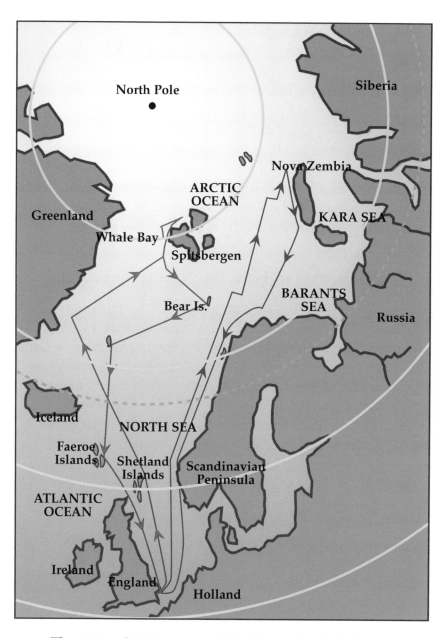

The 1607 and 1608 voyages of the *Hopewell* to Spitsbergen and Nova Zembla while seeking a northern passage to Asia. The 1607 Polar route is in red; the 1608 northeastern route is in purple.

nothing more than congratulations and a renewal of his contract to captain the *Hopewell* again the next year.

The *Hopewell* got within 600 miles of the North Pole but could go no farther. Before turning back to England the ship was nearly crushed by the Great Ice Barrier when chunks of ice were ground together by the waves. Only a change in wind direction saved the ship from drifting into the ice pack. Hudson believed this wind was a miracle, writing in his journal,"The wind was the first from the northwest that has blown in all the days we have sailed in these northern seas." The men cheered loudly when they set sail for England.

The Attempt to Find the Northeast Passage

By early 1608 Hudson's name was known throughout Europe for his exploration, but he turned down a well-paid job to lead whaling expeditions to Spitsbergen, in spite of his wife's protest. He was determined instead to find the Northeast Passage to Asia. He still believed the route would be ice-free farther east.

The *Hopewell* left England again on April 22, 1608. For the first twelve hours of the voyage they were carried 63 miles by the Norwegian current. During an Arctic summer there are twenty-four hours of sunlight, which Hudson recorded in his log. By June 8 he noted the water was dark blue, indicating ice was not far away. They reached Nova Zembla at the end of June. Some of the men went ashore and found the tracks of large bears, deer, and foxes. They also saw walruses swimming in the calm seas.

By early July, however, it became clear the waterway was too shallow to sail through to the east shore of Nova Zembla. Ice was also blocking any Northeast Passage. Once Hudson and his crew realized their mission was impossible, they looked for something valuable to bring the Muscovy Company, as they had done with whales the previous year.

On June 30 all of the crew, except Hudson and his son, set out to hunt walruses for their valuable tusks, hides and blubber. They found it difficult and uncertain hunting. The walruses could dive in the water and easily escape, so they only got one.

Hudson's crew hoped walrus tusks, hide, and blubber would make money for the Muscovy Company.

Captain Hudson recorded all the usual information in his log about the voyage to Nova Zembla, such as water depth, latitude and weather conditions. But on June 15 came this startling entry: he noted the sighting of mermaids, "close to the ship's side, looking earnestly on the men." Were these porpoises or seals, or just a product of his imagination? Sailors of the time were uneducated and very superstitious. They expected to see and were ready to believe in strange sights in unknown waters. People today still search for the unexplained, such as the Loch Ness Monster and Bigfoot, and some even claim to have seen them!

After more than three months in the Arctic, Hudson was still determined to find a northern passage to Asia. By the end of July the Arctic summer with its long hours of daylight was ending, and Hudson needed candlelight to write in his journal. He no longer described the landscape and animals of the region as he turned west toward the Davis Strait south of Labrador.

Meanwhile, his crew became increasingly nervous as they realized the ship was not sailing south back to England, but west across the Atlantic. First Mate Juet challenged Captain Hudson about the ship's course and strongly hinted that the men might not obey orders. Hudson decided to ease their fears and prevent a possible mutiny. He recorded in his log on August 7 that he "gave a certificate of his free and willing return, without being forced by the crew." This event possibly predicted Hudson's future fate. In a later voyage Robert Juet would lead a successful mutiny. Henry Hudson possessed great courage and excellent seamanship and navigational skills. However, the voyage of 1608 showed his weak leadership ability, his obsession with finding a northern water route to Asia, and a lack of understanding and compassion for his crew. Hudson was not a good judge of character, and his lack of judgment would bring his downfall.

When the *Hopewell* finally reached England on August 26, 1608, there was no mention made of an attempted mutiny, possibly for fear of punishment. Crowds cheered the *Hopewell*'s return, and King James met with Hudson in a formal audience. However, the Muscovy Company was losing interest in Hudson's attempts to find a shorter waterway to Asia. The company was now making good profits from whaling in Spitsbergen, but no profits from the voyage to Nova Zembla.

Hudson felt he had failed in his mission, but in reality his reputation as a mapmaker and knowledgeable navigator had spread throughout Europe. England's rivals, France and the new country of Holland, were now eager to find a passage to the riches of Asia. In autumn 1608, a representative of Holland's Dutch East India Company met Hudson and offered a handsome reward to whomever discovered a new, shorter northern route.

Chapter 4
1609: An Eventful Year

The events that took place during the summer and fall of 1609 were important in the history of New York State and neighboring Vermont. Samuel de Champlain supported his Indian allies on a raid along the shores of Lake Champlain. The French used their arquebuses (a type of gun fired with a slow-burning match cord) to help defeat the Mohawk Iroquois. This began a French-Iroquois conflict that would last well over 150 years. This conflict eventually helped bring the end of New France in North America.

During this same year Henry Hudson, sailing for Holland, traveled up the "River of Mountains," later named for

A replica of Champlain's ship, *Le Don de Dieu*, at the 1909 tercentenary celebration of the European discovery of Lake Champlain.

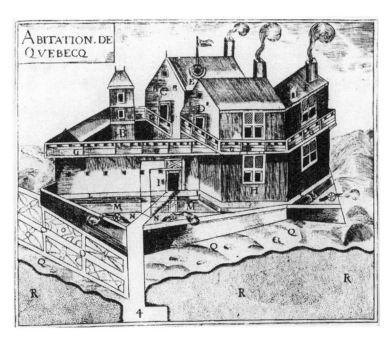

Champlain's drawing of Quebec Habitation from Les *Voyages*, 1613. It would remain a seasonal trading post for many years.

him, in New York State. He failed in his quest to find the Northwest Passage, but as a result of his exploration and discoveries, the Dutch began to settle in the Hudson River Valley. It often happens that accidental or unintended discoveries turn out to have the most influence on history. This proved to be true for both Champlain and Hudson.

Samuel de Champlain's ship, *Le Don de Dieu* ("Gift of God"), arrived at the trading center of Tadoussac on the north shore of the St. Lawrence River on June 3, 1608. They discovered Basques from northern Spain were competing with the French fur trade monopoly, and had a brief skirmish with them. Champlain had convinced Sieur de Monts, his superior, to fund the building of a habitation at Quebec. This location was farther inland and hundreds of miles closer to the source of furs than Port Royal. Only a month after

Facing page:
A French soldier with an arquebus (also called a mousquit).

landing at Tadoussac, Champlain's men were hard at work cutting butternut trees for beams to be used for the fortification, which included a moat and drawbridge. The glazed windows had been brought from France on the ship and were transported up the St. Lawrence in smaller boats. The name Quebec came from a Micmac Indian word, *kebec*, meaning "the narrows of a river."

Before the Quebec Habitation was finished, several workmen led by the locksmith, Jean Duval, plotted to betray and murder Champlain and sell the new fort to the Basques.

They planned to return home as rich men, but Champlain learned of the plot in time. The conspirators were put on trial. The ringleader, Duval, was hung, and the other three were sent back to France in chains to receive punishment. Champlain had dealt swiftly with this unsuccessful mutiny attempt, and he was never threatened by mutiny again, unlike his fellow explorer Henry Hudson.

The winter of 1608-09 was especially harsh, with bitter cold and deep snow at times. The settlement began to run out of food. Their Indian allies, the Montagnais, had provided a supply of smoked eels, but before the end of January those were gone. Both the French and the Indians suffered from hunger. The Montagnais were so desperate they killed and ate their dogs and even rotten meat set out for fox bait. By February, 18 of the 24 Frenchmen had scurvy. Ten of those died, and three more died of dysentery. Champlain himself was ill with scurvy. By spring only 8 of the French were still alive.

When April arrived, the survivors nibbled the new shoots of spring plants, and scurvy gradually disappeared. Supply ships from France arrived with food, trade goods, and additional men. Although the king had not extended the fur trade monopoly, de Monts still intended to finance the Quebec Habitation.

One positive thing came out of the hard winter. Two young Frenchmen, Etienne Brule and Nicolas Marsolet, became interested in learning the Algonquin language and way of life. This was a major benefit in communicating with local Indians. Champlain was not good at languages himself, and he had not brought an interpreter along. Before now he had communicated using a few Montagnais words and gestures, and the Montagnais had probably learned a few French words.

In June 1609, Champlain had to decide whether to remain neutral in the long ongoing war between the Algonquins and the Iroquois. He wanted to protect the French fur trade if possible. He finally decided to keep the promise made six years earlier to help the Algonquins. Several hundred Indian allies met at Quebec for five days of feasting and ceremonies before heading south into Iroquois country. For the first time Champlain met the Huron, who spoke the Iroquois language. The first Frenchmen to see these Indians named them "Huron," because they wore their coarse black hair in a ridge on top of their heads. It reminded the French of a boar's head, for which the French word is "hure."

At the mouth of the Richelieu River a number of Indians took their trade goods of iron pots and glass beads, and returned home. This left only 60 Indians, including Huron, Montagnais and other Algonquins, and three Frenchmen, including Champlain. The French wore metal armor and carried heavy arquebuses.

By July 14 the war party had reached a huge, 125-mile lake that was the source of the Richelieu River. Champlain later named it after himself, Lake Champlain. He and the other two Frenchmen are thought to be the first Europeans to have set foot in present-day New York State. For two weeks they paddled south. Champlain noted that on the eastern shore were "very high mountains on the tops of which there was snow." Perhaps he did see snow in July, or perhaps it was an outcropping of white marble on Mount Mansfield in Vermont. As they drew nearer to enemy territory, they traveled by night, and slept and hid in the woods by day. It took over two weeks to reach Mohawk territory. One time the Indians asked Champlain what he had dreamed, and he told them he had seen Iroquois drowning in a lake. This dream encouraged his allies, as their culture believed strongly in the importance of dreams.

On the evening of July 29 a Mohawk war party was paddling north in their heavy elm bark canoes and spotted the invaders. The two groups traded insults and boasted about their expected victories all through the night. They quickly came ashore and used their stone axes to built a barricade of tree trunks.

At dawn Champlain's group came ashore unhindered and made their battle formation. The Mohawks outnumbered them three to one, with over 200 warriors. The two opposing groups approached each other, and Champlain's Indian allies surrounded him until they were within striking distance. Champlain then walked within thirty yards of the Mohawks and fired his arquebus. He aimed for three chiefs, easily identified by their feather headdresses. Three of the four lead balls found their targets. Two chiefs were killed and the third died later of his wounds.

While Champlain reloaded, the other two Frenchmen were ready to fire from where they were concealed in the tree line. Champlain recorded, "One of my companions fired a shot within the woods, which astonished them so much that, seeing their chiefs dead, they lost courage and took to flight, abandoning the field and their fort, and fleeing into the depths of the forest, whither I pursued them and laid low still more of them." Sixteen of Champlain's allies were wounded but no lives were lost. The Algonquin allies took twelve Mohawks prisoner. Champlain was horrified to witness the torture and deaths of these prisoners. He

Champlain's sketch of the encounter with the Mohawks.

Champlain recorded many details in his sketch of the battle at Lake Champlain. He is in the center, wearing full armor and firing his arquebus. This is the only illustration of Champlain actually done during his lifetime. The three chiefs are shown mortally wounded on the ground, and the two Frenchmen are firing their arquebuses from the woods. The boats on the left are birch bark canoes. The ones on the right are the heavier Mohawk elm bark canoes. All the boats somewhat resemble French river boats, possibly because Champlain drew what was most familiar. The Indians are shown fighting with no clothing on, a detail that was not historically accurate. Some historians believe Champlain followed the custom of artists of his time, to show Indians naked so they could be easily told apart from the Europeans. The palm trees are also inaccurate. These certainly did not grow along the shores of Lake Champlain. Why did Champlain include them? Possibly he wanted to make the setting more exotic, or was remembering earlier voyages to the West Indies.

refused to take part but had no influence over his allies' cruel treatment, which was their custom.

The Battle of Lake Champlain was won in spite of overwhelming odds because of a new weapon, the arquebus. It changed the tactics of warfare between Europeans and Indians. Champlain, in effect, had broken the rules of warfare that Indians had used for centuries. Now faced with a superior weapon, the Indians resorted to raids and surprise attacks against their better-armed enemy. From that time on, Indians tried to obtain those "thunder tubes" by trading, stealing, or killing.

After the battle, Champlain's allies celebrated with singing and dancing, and they feasted on cornmeal left behind by their enemies. They had no desire to pursue the fleeing Mohawks. Soon a flotilla of birch bark canoes headed north, traveling about 120 miles in only two days to return home in glory with their enemies' scalps. Champlain's participation in this battle earned him respect among both the Indians and the French, as a brave man who keeps his word.

Champlain had little time after the battle to explore Lake Champlain farther south. He mentions that he saw the rapids at the outlet to another large lake (present-day Lake George), but his exploration ended with the battle. Some historians think that if he had not taken sides by backing the Algonquin alliance, he might have been able to explore farther west and south. He might have arrived on Manhattan Island ahead of Henry Hudson, who came there a few months later. Champlain took a calculated risk to help his allies, hoping to explore new territory. Unfortunately Champlain backed the losing side. In the end, the Iroquois defeated the Huron and controlled the fur trade.

When Champlain returned to the Quebec Habitation, he was busy directing improvements to the fort until he left for France again in September. About a month later he presented King Henry IV souvenirs from his adventures, including the skull of a monster garfish from Lake Champlain and a belt made with porcupine quills. The king refused to extend the fur trade monopoly for de Monts' company, probably because the hatters were complaining about the high price of the beaver pelts used for making felt hats. De Monts decided to fund the company himself, since the Quebec fur trade was so profitable. He hoped Champlain's victory over the Mohawks might further increase profits. Two ships set sail from France on April 8, 1610, with eleven men and supplies for the next winter. With the help of a strong east wind, the ships made the passage to the Grand Banks of Newfoundland in a record eleven days.

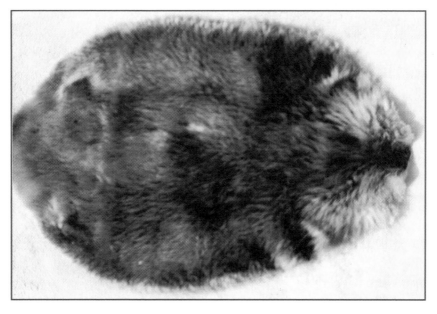

Beaver pelts, similar to the thousands sent to France. Hatters used the beaver hairs to make felt for hats.

Chapter 5
Henry Hudson
Returns to North America

The V.O.C. flag flown by Hudson's ship. From a 1909 postcard commemorating the 300th anniversary of Hudson's arrival in what would become New York State.

Holland's Dutch East India Company, which was very interested in finding a northern passage to the spices of Asia, approached Hudson in the fall 1608.

The United Dutch East India Company, or V.O.C. in Dutch, hoped finding a new route would avoid conflict and competition with other countries like Spain, Portugal, and England. Around this time a treaty was signed in which Spain formally recognized the independence of the Dutch Republic, and the new country of Holland was formed. The Dutch East India Company was far wealthier than the Muscovy Company for whom Hudson had sailed previously.

The Dutch East India Company directors met with Hudson and listened to his experiences, but they were hesitant to grant him a contract. They thought it was too late in the year to set sail for the Arctic. Henry Hudson then consulted Peter Plancius, a famous Dutch geographer who lived in the capital, The Hague. They spent hours studying the latest maps and discussing theories, such as the possibility of a northwest passage along the coast of North America, south of Labrador. With the support of Plancius and one of the Dutch East India Company's directors, Hudson contacted King Henry IV of France. King Henry IV already had interest in the development of New France in the St. Lawrence River Valley. But before King Henry IV could make Hudson an offer, the Dutch East India Company got wind of it. They did not want to see France gain any advantage. They summoned Hudson to Amsterdam in January. This time he brought his own interpreter and signed a contract that specifically stated he was to look for a northeast passage north of Nova Zembla, not the Northwest Passage of which he had always dreamed. The contract also provided a salary of 800 guilders (about $350). In the event of his death, his wife Katherine would receive 200 guilders. It also required Hudson and his family to live in Holland, and forbade him to work for any other company. What if the Dutch East India Company had delayed a little longer in offering the contract to Henry Hudson? The history of the New World might have turned out quite differently, with both Hudson and Samuel de Champlain representing France, and searching for the elusive water passage to Asia at the same time.

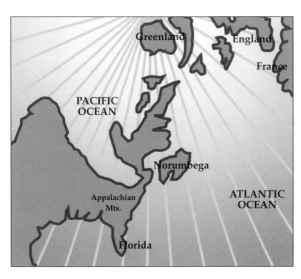

Map of North America based on information from early explorers and Indians, showing the Pacific only a few hundred miles from the Atlantic.

(Adapted from a 16th-century map.)

Before leaving Holland, Hudson received a letter and some maps from Captain John Smith in Jamestown, Virginia. Based on information from Indians and earlier explorations, Smith believed the Great Lakes were a single body of salt water stretching across North America. Smith thought Hudson's shortcut to Asia could be found by following a river somewhere north of Virginia that would lead to this great body of water and to the Pacific. No one had any idea of the size of the continent.

The Dutch East India Company provided Hudson with a small 60-ton, flat-bottomed and clumsy-looking ship called the *Half Moon*, and a crew of 18-20 men. Hudson was a little doubtful about the ship's seaworthiness. He may have requested a bigger or better one, but the Dutch East India Company refused. He did order extra masts and sails, which the company refused to pay for, so he charged them.

Roughly half of the crew were Dutch sailors, and the rest were English. No list of the crew members has survived, but it is known that Henry Hudson's teenage son John, John Colman, who had been on the Spitzbergen voyage, and Robert Juet were part of the crew. Juet's journal of the 1609 voyage became a main source of information. After Juet's disloyalty on Hudson's previous voyage, it is a mystery why Hudson rehired him.

Hudson spoke little Dutch and had to rely on his interpreter to help with the hiring. From the start Colman and Juet were not impressed with the crew. There was friction over matters such as food. For example, the Dutch sailors preferred salted herring, while the English seamen expected pickled beef.

The *Half Moon* set sail on April 6, 1609, after numerous delays, some deliberate on Hudson's part. He ignored the company's orders to leave in March. He felt it was too early and the northern seas would still be ice-filled and too dangerous for his small wooden ship. There was little fanfare at their departure. Almost immediately the ship hit a severe storm. Many of the crew became seasick. Hudson proved his seamanship by lashing himself to the quarterdeck and keeping the ship on course.

Hudson may have been tempted to head west toward North America, but he had signed a contract and sworn an oath to go to the Arctic. By early May they reached the northern cape of Scandinavia. It was extremely cold, and the Dutch sailors especially suffered terribly. Too late, Hudson learned they had no experience with cold climates. They had sailed in the tropical waters of the East Indies. Consequently, the Dutch sailors avoided outdoor chores whenever possible, leaving them to the English crew members. This caused more resentment.

Fights broke out between the two groups of sailors, leading to near mutiny. Captain Hudson seemed unable to deal with the necessary discipline. To make matters worse, on May 19 Juet wrote in his journal, "We observed the sun having a slake." *Slake* was slang for dirt. He possibly was referring to a thin layer of clouds shadowing the sun. Whatever it was, it disturbed the superstitious crew. Some muttered about the end of the world.

Hudson used this event to his advantage. He offered the crew a choice: to return home with their mission a failure, or try to seek a western sea passage to Asia. He suggested if they returned to Amsterdam, they might face charges of mutiny. The penalty for mutiny was hanging. Hudson put it to a vote, and the crew voted unanimously in favor of sailing west. Hudson also mentioned two possible routes. One was by way of the Davis Strait and the Furious Overfall, northwest of Labrador. The other was to follow the suggestions of Captain John Smith and sail farther south to look for a river that would lead to the Pacific Ocean. Hudson opted for the second choice. He knew his crew did not handle cold weather well.

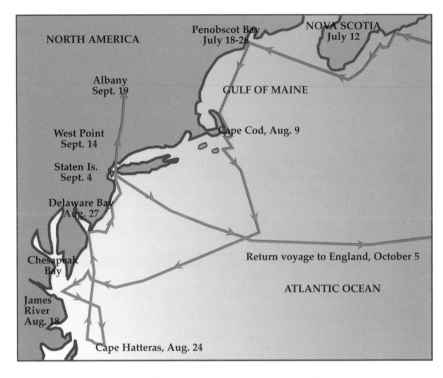

Map of the 1609 route taken by the *Half Moon* along the eastern coast of North America.

Both the English and Dutch sailors became more cheerful at the change of plans, and they worked together enthusiastically to change course. The little ship hit a severe storm on May 25, but survived, and the strong winds helped push them along. They reached the Faeroe Islands a few days later. They stopped for water and to barter for supplies with the natives before continuing on.

After barely surviving another violent storm in which they lost a mast, the *Half Moon* reached the Grand Banks off Newfoundland on July 3. Here they met a French fishing fleet, which signaled these were their fishing grounds. So the *Half Moon* proceeded a little farther south, and one of the Dutch sailors, an expert fisherman, suggested they try fishing. In just five hours they caught 118 large codfish and more herring than they could handle. Hudson wanted to use their salt supply mainly to preserve the codfish, which was more profitable in Europe. The Dutch sailors grumbled, but ate their fill of fresh herring and kept a supply alive by towing it in nets behind the ship.

A white sandy beach was sighted at dawn on July 12. The crew begged to go ashore, so Hudson chose half of them for a landing party. But to their disappointment, a thick fog rolled in and lasted five days. To keep the impatient crew safely aboard the ship, Hudson told them that the waters were infested with sharks. When the fog briefly cleared, they could see they were anchored in an island cove near the entrance to a bay, later known as Penobscot Bay, Maine. When the fog moved back in, Hudson and the crew heard voices and the splash of canoe paddles. They quickly armed themselves and prepared for an attack. The invaders proved to be six Indians dressed in moccasins and loincloths, and armed only with stone knives. Hudson decided they posed no threat and allowed them on board. To his amazement the leader spoke to them in French, a result of contact with French fur traders and fishermen. These were likely part of the Penobscot branch of the Algonquin Indians. Hudson gave them gifts of beads, blankets, and mirrors, and offered them food. They enjoyed the herring, but refused to eat the ship's hardtack biscuits. Experience had already taught them it was rock hard and not very tasty. Juet recorded, "We gave them trifles and ate and drank with them. They told us there was gold, silver and copper mines close by."

The Indians probably said that because previous European visitors had asked repeatedly about such things. Hudson remained doubtful it was true, reasoning that the French would have already taken anything of real value.

On July 18 Hudson set foot on North American soil for

the first time. The crew had gone ashore to cut down a tree to replace the broken mast. Hudson was awed and amazed at the tall trees and seemingly endless forests. Juet wrote,"We also found a shoal with many lobsters on it and caught 31." The lobster feast must have been very welcome after the monotonous diet aboard ship.

Typical items traded by the Europeans, including glass beads. These were prized by the Indians as they spent long hours making beads from shells by hand.

The next day the Indians returned with beaver skins and other fine furs to trade. The usual trade articles were such things as iron knives, spear points, hatchets, copper kettles, trivets, small mirrors, and beads, but this group only wanted "red gowns." Hudson was puzzled until an elderly Indian stepped forward, dressed in a red woolen nightshirt, no doubt obtained from a French trader. Hudson quickly rounded up similar nightshirts from the crew in exchange for several bales of beaver and fox pelts that would bring high prices in Europe. Hudson had no experience with the fur trade and did not realize that the pelts were much more valuable than the salted cod in the ship's cargo hold. Furs were also much more available than the gold and silver most European explorers hoped for, but failed to find.

Before leaving Penobscot Bay, some of the crew went ashore to smoke some fish. They were not successful, but before returning to the ship they stole a canoe. Later they returned with their firearms and the Indians ran into the woods. The crew then stole the Indians' belongings. Captain Hudson did not discipline the men for this, nor did he try to make peace with the Indians. Instead, Juet recorded, "At five o'clock in the morning we set sail and put out to sea."

From the coast of Maine the *Half Moon* sailed around Cape Cod. Hudson first called it "New Holland," but after consulting his maps, he realized they were on the coast of Cape Cod. It had been named in 1602 for the large number of cod fish there. Some of the men went ashore and returned with bunches of sweet wild grapes and described wild roses blooming. They had arrived during a summer heat wave, which caused them to mistakenly assume the region had a warm climate.

By mid-August they had reached the southernmost point of their voyage, the coast of Virginia. In spite of being near Jamestown, the colony founded by Hudson's friend Captain John Smith, they did not stop to say hello. Foreign ships were not usually welcome in English colonies, and while Hudson and some of his crew might be English, the *Half Moon* was a Dutch ship.

Hudson then began to search seriously for the rumored waterway that would take them across North America to the Pacific Ocean. They sailed north, and by the end of August had reached Delaware Bay. Hudson decided none of the rivers they had seen thus far were deep enough. On

September 2 the *Half Moon* sailed around Sandy Hook in present-day New Jersey and arrived at a "great lake of water." He saw the mouth of the great river that would be named for him, the Hudson River. Henry Hudson was the first to explore it, but he was not the discoverer. That honor goes to Giovanni da Verrazano, an Italian sailing for France, who had found it in 1524.

Chapter 6
Hudson Explores the "River of Mountains"

For the next few days the crew took depth soundings around the shore of Staten Island and netted ten large mullet near the shore. They started up the river, and on September 4 Hudson and crew made their first contact with the Mannahatas and Lenape Indians. The Indians traded green tobacco and Indian wheat, or corn, for iron knives and glass trade beads. Juet mentioned that the Indian wheat made good bread. Hudson and the crew went ashore to explore and found wild plums, berries, grapes, wild celery, and something less welcome, poison ivy. This plant was unfamiliar to them, and one of the Dutch sailors broke out in a rash after touching it.

The Indians told Hudson the river he had seen was very large. Hoping that at last he'd found the route to Asia, Hudson sent John Colman and four others out in a small boat to explore the area south around Manhattan Island. Before they could get back to the ship they were caught in a fog. Juet recorded in his journal that they were attacked by two canoes of Indians. It began to rain and the crew's lamp went out. John Colman was killed with an arrow to the throat, and two others were injured. It became too dark to find the ship. In the morning they returned to the *Half Moon* with Colman's body. He was buried on a point they named Colman's Point in his memory. After this sad and frightening event, Hudson prepared the ship's defenses by boarding up the portholes and readying the cannons to be fired. The men carried firearms, and a watch was posted around the clock.

Hudson was very cautious now about contact with the Indians. On September 9 two large canoes filled with Indians arrived to trade. Hudson had them searched before allowing them aboard. Once the bartering was finished, he hustled them off the ship. Before they had all left he took two as hostages against further attacks. The captives were not well-treated by the crew. The practice of taking Indian captives was not unusual; Giovanni da Verrazano and others had done it in the early 1500s. This did little to build friendly relations between the Indians and later European explorers.

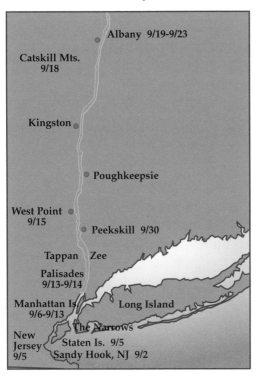

Route of Henry Hudson's 1609 voyage up the Hudson River in search of a northwest passage.

On September 11 the *Half Moon* sailed through the Narrows and into what became New York Harbor. Juet recorded:"It was a very good harbor, with protection from all winds." Over the next few days Indians continued to arrive by canoe to trade. At one point there were 28 canoes. Hudson and crew traded for oysters and beans, but remained distrustful. Juet commented, "We saw their intent of treachery and would not allow any of them to come aboard." By September 13 the ship was near the present-day location of Grant's Tomb, where again Indians came to barter for glass beads and mirrors.

Hudson's historic voyage up the Hudson River began early on the morning of September 13. The ship weighed anchor (brought it up) and set sail on the flood, or high tide. The ocean tides extend about 100 miles up the river, so the Indians called it *Muhheakunnuck,* which meant "great waters constantly in motion." Hudson called it the River of Mountains. They anchored in about five fathoms, or 30 feet, of water that afternoon.

Hudson knew he had found a major waterway, so he made detailed notes and charts. He took depth soundings, tested currents, and recorded navigational hazards such as sandbars and rocks. Hudson also described the high bluffs known as the Palisades that "stretch for approximately 15 miles on the west of the river and are ever a delight to the eye. Behind this natural wall stretches the great forest, which lies like a cloak over most of the New World." He marveled at the abundance of birds and guessed the forests were filled with game. However, he dared not send a landing party ashore for fear of attack.

The *Half Moon* continued slowly northward, passing through the three-mile-wide section of the river later called the Tappan Zee, named after local Indians. Hudson was amazed at the scenic wonders he saw, standing for hours on the quarterdeck, recording the changing width as they went by present-day Peekskill, New York. Hudson believed the river was a strait, or narrow waterway, that would lead to a sea and on to Asia. The ship rode the flood tides all the way

Indians approach the *Half Moon* to trade. The Palisades are in the background. Drawing by Andrew Thompson

to West Point, where they saw high mountains and "the river full of fish."

On September 15 the *Half Moon* sailed an amazing 60 miles, thanks to a strong wind from the south. At this point the two Indian hostages they had taken a few days earlier jumped overboard and swam to shore. They shouted insults before disappearing into the forest. By nightfall the ship had reached the Catskill Mountains. Here they were met by Indians in white birch bark canoes. These Mohican Indians of the Catskill region were more welcoming and less hostile than the ones they had met farther south. They paddled out to barter their Indian corn, pumpkins, and tobacco.

A few days later on September 18 Hudson was invited by a local chief to a feast in his honor. The food included roast pigeon and dog meat, a dish Hudson very reluctantly tried. He did not find it as unpleasant as he feared, and commented it tasted like pork. When Hudson made ready to leave, his Indian hosts broke arrows to indicate they meant no harm.

Hudson described the homes of these Indians. They were "dwelling together in large circular houses well-constructed of oak bark (with) a pit lined with stones to cook meals." Their skill with tools and weapons made of shell and stone also impressed Hudson, and in spite of Juet's mistrust, he gave them some iron knives. After observing their crops of maize (corn), squash and beans, and noting the abundance of fish and game, Hudson suggested that if his own people were to come and settle there, "they would soon transform this wilderness into a Paradise where no man ever need go hungry."

Breaking arrows as a sign of friendship.
Drawing by Andrew Thompson

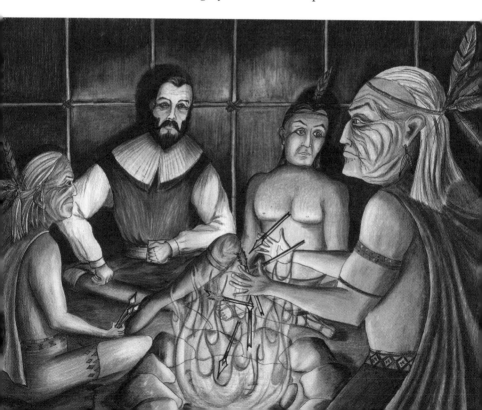

The modern-day replica of the *Half Moon* near Peekskilll, New York.

By September 19 the *Half Moon* had sailed 150 miles up the Hudson River and anchored near present-day Albany. Hudson sent out the gig (small boat) and some crew to take soundings and explore. The men returned with discouraging news: the river narrowed upstream and became increasingly shallow. Before continuing on, a group of Indians arrived from a large village called Schenectadea. They gave Hudson wampum (strings of clam shell beads assembled in patterns for belts and jewelry), tobacco, and venison in return for knives and woolen blankets.

The next day Hudson decided to try the route north once more. This time the crew added a sail to make the small boat go faster. When they returned, the news was disastrous. They had been able to go only about 12 miles north of Albany near present-day Waterford. The river then became so narrow and shallow the *Half Moon* would not be able to navigate it. Their voyage had reached a dead end. On September 23 the *Half Moon* turned around and headed back down the river.

With the arrival of fall, Hudson knew they needed to reach the open sea while the weather was still favorable. Strong winds drove the ship onto mud banks several times. The ship was prevented from sailing south until the high tide came upriver and floated them free.

Unfortunately before leaving present-day Peekskill, Hudson ran into trouble with the Indians. A band of Indians approached to trade, and one of them sneaked through a porthole in Juet's cabin and stole a pillow, two shirts and a sword. He was spotted and shot and killed. Juet, eager to regain his belongings, led a pursuit in the gig. He did get his things back, but Hudson, fearing an attack, quickly ordered the ship to set sail.

Hudson was right to be worried. The next morning a large party of Indians in canoes, including one of the escaped hostages, approached. Half of the crew readied weapons while the rest worked frantically to get the ship up to maximum speed. Up ahead they could see about 100 warriors ready to attack from a point of land. Amidst a rain of arrows, Hudson ordered the cannon to be fired. Several Indians were killed and the rest scattered. The *Half Moon* sailed out of arrow range and did not anchor again until well south, near present-day Hoboken, New Jersey.

Hudson posted guards and remained on deck all night himself. In the morning heavy fog prevented further progress. The tide and currents made the ship drift, so, in spite of the poor visibility, they continued downstream where they anchored for 24 hours, all the while fearful of being attacked. The next morning the fog had cleared and the *Half Moon* could depart.

Hudson and his crew had no way of knowing the importance of their discoveries. Holland remained interested primarily in the fur trade for the next 12 years. It was not until 1624 that the Dutch got around to establishing the permanent settlement of New Netherlands on the southern tip of Manhattan Island. Hudson's explorations led to the Dutch claim of this area. It would some day become a population and commercial center, and one of the world's largest cities, New York City. All Hudson knew was that they had failed in their mission to find a water route to Asia.

Before setting sail in early October Hudson asked his crew if they wanted to winter over in North America and try again in the spring. Of course, Hudson himself wanted to stay for the winter, but the rest of the crew overwhelmingly wanted to go home. Hudson could not blame them. Their supplies were nearly gone, and facing winter with little food and no ale did not appeal to anyone. Hudson then suggested they winter in Iceland, to which the men agreed. However they actually landed in Dartmouth, England on November 7, 1609, about a month after leaving North America.

Upon reaching England, Hudson contacted his Dutch employers and asked to return to North America again to seek the Northwest Passage. He requested more money and replacement of some crew members. Before anything could be settled, King James of England had Hudson placed under house arrest, and forbade the crew to leave England. King James did not want Holland to benefit from Hudson's discoveries. Thus ended Hudson's third voyage in 1609.

Chapter 7
Champlain Helps his Indian Allies and Explores the Interior 1610-1616

When Champlain returned to Quebec from France in May, 1610, he found the colony in good shape and free of scurvy. The winter had been mild so the men had been able to get enough fresh meat. Champlain was eager to renew his search for the "great salt sea" that would lead to the riches of Asia. However, his Huron and Montagnais allies were equally eager for him to join in a war party against some Mohawk Iroquois, who had come to get revenge for their loss in the 1609 battle. With the help of the French and their arquebuses, the Mohawks were defeated for a second time on June 19, 1610. Champlain's drawing of the battle shows his Indian allies advancing under cover of wood shields covered with deerskins. During the heat of battle Champlain was hit, and recorded. "an arrow split the tip of my ear and pierced my neck." He removed it himself and seemed almost as bothered by the swarms of mosquitoes as by his wounds.

When Champlain returned to Quebec two days later, he was met by the sad news his friend King Henry IV had been assassinated in France. Henry's nine-year-old son, Louis XIII, replaced him on the throne. The boy king's mother, Marie de Medici, was regent for her son, ruling on his behalf until he was older. Champlain worried that Marie cared little about the Quebec Habitation, so he decided he needed to return to France immediately and secure support for the colony. He left just sixteen men in Quebec.

One of the ways Champlain hoped to gain influence at

court was through marriage to the daughter of a court official. Marriages at that time were usually arranged for political or financial reasons. On December 30, 1610, 40-year-old Samuel de Champlain married 12- year-old Helene Boulle, whose brother had been at the Port Royal Habitation. Champlain received a considerable dowry. He used a large portion to set up a house and servants for his young wife. The rest he used to outfit his next expedition.

Champlain's sketch of the June, 1610 Battle with the Mohawks from his *Les Voyages*, 1613.

By March 1611, Champlain had left for the New World, leaving his child bride at home. Of all his twenty-three voyages across the Atlantic, this was the worst and longest, over ten weeks. Ice and fog made the journey slow and dangerous. They did not arrive at Tadoussac until May.

Upon arrival Champlain discovered the price of fur pelts had been driven up by the arrival of independent fur traders. At this time France was importing about 15,000 beaver skins each year. The traders paid the Indians less than fifty cents in goods for each pelt. When the furs reached France, they were sold for ten to twenty times the amount paid.

In the summer of 1611 Champlain met his allies on the island of Montreal, the largest annual gathering place for the exchange of furs. They feasted and the French traded iron pots, beads and trinkets for a variety of animal furs. By now the Indians were calling them *agnon ha*, "the iron people" because of all the French trade goods made of iron. Champlain impressed the Indians with his bravery in shooting the La Chine Rapids in a canoe. In spite of his requests, his allies were reluctant to take him north into the interior, perhaps fearing they would lose some of their fur trade. So Champlain decided to return to France again to gather further support for his explorations. He left a young man named Nicolas Vignau behind with the Indians to learn more about the interior water routes.

Champlain was desperate to save the struggling New France. Once back in France he rose in position and prestige. Prince de Conde made Champlain his deputy. This gave Champlain the authority to govern New France. He served in this position for more than 19 years, starting in 1612. His stay in France was very successful. His company was granted a new fur trade monopoly. Champlain also published the first volume of his book, *Les Voyages*.

Nicolas Vignau returned to France and told Champlain how he had traveled up the Ottawa River and had reached "the Northern Salt Sea," Hudson Bay. Vignau related he had seen the wreck of an English ship, possibly from Henry Hudson's voyage in 1610. He also had heard stories of an English boy, perhaps John Hudson, joining an Indian tribe. Vignau's tales of his adventures made Champlain eager to return to the New World.

The French authorities were convinced the British pres-

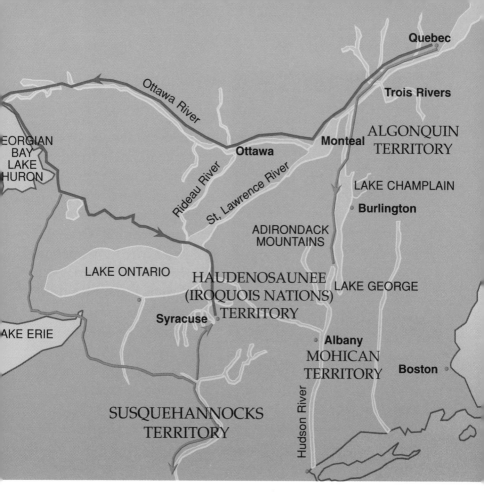

The route Champlain took up the Ottawa River, 1613 and 1615, and on Lake Champlain in 1609, while attempting to find a passage to the Pacific Ocean.

ence was a threat to New France and their control of the fur trade, so Champlain was given the task of visiting Hudson Bay himself. By 1613 he was back in Montreal, awaiting his allies. Just a few Indians came, however, because of disputes with illegal fur traders. Only one Indian agreed to be his guide, and Champlain had to carry his own canoe on portages, when the waterway could not be navigated. They started out on May 27, 1613, with four Frenchmen in the group, including Vignau. At one point along the Ottawa River, Champlain was nearly caught in a whirlpool. Farther

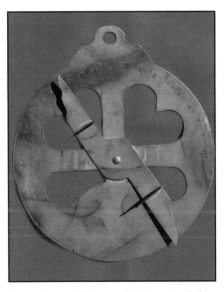

A replica of Champlain's astrolabe.

on they met a party of 15 Algonquin canoes coming downstream. The Indians warned the French of dangers ahead and provided Champlain with another guide. Eventually they reached the future site of Canada's capital, Ottawa.

The expedition encountered numerous portages and other difficulties until they reached a slender chain of lakes. {Along this route in 1867, a farm boy found a bronze mariner's astrolabe, dated 1603. It may have been lost by Champlain 250 years earlier.)

After weeks of a long, difficult journey, Champlain began to doubt that Vignau had ever made it as far as Hudson Bay. The Indian guide swore he'd never gone any farther north and called Vignau a liar, threatening to tear his heart out. Vignau confessed he'd made up the story of seeing an English shipwreck. Champlain then decided to abandon the journey to Hudson Bay. They were back at the La Chine Rapids by June 7, 1613.

Champlain went back to France again in the fall of 1613. He convinced influential merchants to form the Company of Canada to help New France compete with the English and the Dutch. The English had destroyed Port Royal in Acadia, and the Dutch were beginning to trade with the Indians at Fort Orange (Albany, New York).

Shortly after Champlain returned to New France in 1615, he set out from Montreal Island with young Etienne Brule for the homeland of the Huron in the present-day province of Ontario. This time they traveled 75 miles farther up the Ottawa River than they had in 1613. Finally they reached Georgian Bay in Lake Huron, the "freshwater sea" that Indians had described to Cartier in 1535. Before reaching Lake Huron, Champlain met 300 Algonquins calling themselves "Outaouais," from which the name Ottawa came. Their chief drew Champlain a map with charcoal. The Indians were there to gather and dry blueberries for the winter.

The French travelers reached Cahiague, near present-day Orillia, Ontario, on August 17, 1615. At this major village in Huronia they were welcomed "with great joy and gladness by all the savages of the country." The Huron were planning an attack on a fortified Onondaga Iroquois village south of Oneida Lake in present-day New York State. Their allies, the Susquehannocks, lived south of the Iroquois and had promised to help the Huron in a simultaneous raid. The Huron were delighted at the prospect of help from the French with their arquebuses.

On September 8, 1615, Etienne Brule set out to meet the Susquehannocks at the Susquehanna River. The main war party of several hundred Indians and about twenty French paddled across the northeast end of Lac St. Louis (Lake Ontario) into what is now northern New York State. They came ashore near Henderson Harbor and hid their canoes in the woods. They followed the lake shore to the mouth of the Salmon River and reached the area where the village of Pulaski is today. They passed overland through Oswego County, noting "a very pleasing and fine country, watered by numerous small streams." On October 9 they captured a party of eleven Onondagas fishing on the shore of Oneida Lake near Brewerton. Several young men were able to escape and warn their village, however. Champlain was distressed by the torture of the captives and threatened to stop helping his allies in battle. On October 10 the war party reached the Onondaga village and found their enemies were ready behind the thirty-foot walls with stones and water to throw down from a platform.

The Huron chiefs insisted on attacking immediately but Champlain disagreed. Drawing upon his experience with European siege warfare, Champlain directed building a taller siege tower to overlook the walls. This tower, from which the French fired their arquebuses, did help force the defenders back from their platform.

Champlain's drawing of the attack on the Onondaga village, from his *Les Voyages*.

The battle did not go as well as expected, however. The Huron tried to set fire to the fort, but it was on the side of the fort away from the wind. The fires were easily extinguished by the Onondagas. A rain of arrows and stones further discouraged the attackers. Even though the Frenchmen, armed with arquebuses, wounded or killed many, the Huron allies retreated when several of their chiefs were wounded. Champlain also took arrows to his knee and leg. The Huron and French moved back to the woods, built a makeshift fort, and waited for the Susquehannocks to arrive. They had been promised 500 warriors, but after four days none showed up. The French and Huron had no choice but to quit and go home. Champlain had to be carried all the way back to Lake Ontario in a basket. They later learned that the Susquehannocks belatedly arrived to find the Onondagas celebrating their victory. Etienne Brule was captured, but managed to escape to tell Champlain his tale.

This defeat by the Onondaga Iroquois proved that the French were not invincible, even with their arquebuses, and victory was not a sure thing. Champlain may have preferred peace between his allies and the Iroquois, but he finally realized that war parties were their way of life. He could not know that in this long rivalry between the two, in less than 40 years the Huron would lose control of the fur trade once and for all to the Iroquois/Haudenosaunee.

As the Huron allies retreated through northern New York State, they fished and hunted for deer. Champlain's drawing shows how the Indians herded deer into V-shaped traps and killed them with spears. In about a month they had slaughtered 120 deer for hides and meat to get them through the winter.

During the journey back Champlain slept on a bed of hemlock branches spread over the ground. When his leg injuries healed, he carried a twenty-pound pack. He spent the winter of 1615-16 in Huronia, and recorded many details of life there. He enjoyed the cornmeal bread and commented that "dogs are in demand at their feasts." He

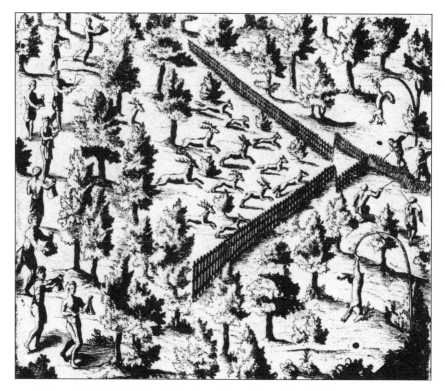

Champlain's sketch of the deer hunt from his *Les Voyages*, 1613.

considered Indian parents too lenient and wrote, "[they] never punish their children so they become so naughty. . .they often strike their mothers."

Champlain did not return to the fur trading center at La Chine Rapids until June. His journey and stay with the Huron had convinced him that the North American continent was far wider and the Pacific Ocean much farther away than previously thought. This was a turning point for Champlain; he began to turn his energies to promoting the development of New France. However, he never stopped believing the Northwest Passage would be found.

Chapter 8
Champlain, the Father of New France

By early September 1616, Champlain was back in France. He was now about 45 years old, and he had made his last trip into the interior of North America. He would now spend the rest of his life traveling back and forth across the Atlantic to promote the growth of New France. He also sought support from the king to defend the colony against the English and the Iroquois.

During the last nineteen years of his life, Champlain never gave up his dream of seeing Quebec become a wealthy trading center on the St. Lawrence. He hoped to see ships bringing the riches of Asia. France seemed content with the money brought in by the fur trade and fishing, however, and Quebec grew very slowly. For years only the arrival of the annual supply ships kept the settlement from starvation. Only one Frenchman came to farm, Louis Herbert. It was not until 1624 that large land grants began to attract more people as settlers and farmers. In 1624 Quebec had only 51 inhabitants, and even by the time of Champlain's death in 1635, there were only 200 people living there. Meanwhile, the populations of the English and Dutch colonies were reaching the thousands.

During these years of struggle, Champlain made the best of the situation and continued to promote improvements. He built the first road in Canada, leading from the Habitation to the top of the Rock in Quebec. During the summer of 1620, his wife Helene, aged twenty-two, arrived and stayed in New France for four years. Young Helene was used to a comfortable life in Paris, and she must have been shocked at the primitive and dilapidated condition of the barn-like building that was their home. Champlain had ordered improvements made, but it was a hard life for her, surrounded by wilderness, with few comforts and the constant threat of Indian attacks. The other inhabitants were mostly rough fur traders, and there were few other women. Little is known of her life there, but history records Helene Champlain became godmother to Pierre Desportes' daughter in 1620.

The Mohawk Iroquois and Montagnais signed a peace treaty in 1623, which eased fear of attack while Helene was still in Quebec. In the fall of 1624 Samuel de Champlain sailed back to France with Helene, who was no doubt very thankful to return to the luxuries of Paris. She never returned to the New World again.

When Champlain came back to Quebec in 1626, he found little had changed. Supplies from France had run out and the settlement was again facing a shortage of food. Louis Herbert was still the only farmer, raising food on his 13 acres of land. The King and trading companies still thought of New France as a "string of summertime trading posts," with a small population. During the winter of 1626-27, the settlers survived only because the local Indians brought them moose meat.

In the spring Champlain heard from nearby Indians who had visited Albany that the Dutch were encouraging Champlain's Indian allies to join a war party against the Mohawk Iroquois. The Mohawks, in turn, were trying to wipe out the Mohicans with whom the Dutch had traded for years. Champlain and his brother-in-law, Eustace Boulle, tried to convince their Indian allies not to break the 1623 treaty that they had worked so hard to achieve. In the end the Mohawks were victorious over the Mohicans.

In 1628 came the news that France and England were at war. English ships blockaded the St. Lawrence. The English commander sent Basque messengers to demand the surrender of Quebec. Champlain, hoping for a relief fleet from France, tried to bluff and refused. In reality the settlement was in bad shape; they had only 50 pounds of gunpowder left and little food. Unfortunately, the expected fleet was defeated, and Quebec was in for a terrible time. They foraged for roots and berries and went moose hunting, but with little food stored and no relief in sight, the settlement was facing starvation.

In July 1629, the English came ashore carrying a white flag. By now Champlain had no choice but to surrender. The English commanders granted Champlain favorable terms of surrender. The French could keep their personal weapons and belongings and would be transported to England. In return, the English took over the fort and the 4,000 beaver pelts stored there. Champlain was dismayed to see Etienne Brule among the English. Brule had betrayed them and helped the English seize Quebec.

The previous January some starving Montagnais had come to Quebec begging for food, and they left behind three young girls whom Champlain had had baptized Foy (Faith), Esperance (Hope), and Charite (Charity). Champlain treated these girls as his own daughters and saw to their religious education. He intended to take them to France for his childless wife Helene to raise, but a dispute arose with the English commander, who refused to allow them to board the ship. They were left behind in Quebec.

By the time the English ships reached Plymouth, England, in October 1629, the war between England and France was over. Champlain was allowed to move freely in England. He spent five weeks in London trying to work out the details of the treaty. It was finally signed in March 1630, and it provided that Canada and Acadia would be returned to France. For his part, King Louis XIII had to repay an overdue debt. Except for the inconvenience to Champlain and the other French from Quebec, it was a good bargain. However, while the negotiations were dragging on, the English were making good profits from transporting thousands of beaver pelts to England.

Prior to the war with England, King Louis XIII's advisor, Cardinal Richelieu, created a larger, more powerful trading company called The Hundred Associates. It was granted a fur trade monopoly so long as they sent 4,000 colonists, excluding Protestants, to New France within fifteen years. This had been set up just as the English were trying to capture Quebec. After the war, Richelieu promoted settlement through large land grants, called the "seigneurial system." This brought French peasants to New France.

Champlain kept his position as the King's and company's lieutenant in New France, but history does not record that he ever received any personal recognition from them. France was losing

A Monument to the "Father of New France" in present-day Quebec.

interest in its colony in North America and its founder, Champlain, "the Father of New France." France was now looking to the East Indies and West Indies for future glory.

When the French finally regained control of Quebec in July 1632, the settlement was in bad shape. The Habitation had been burned down. There were drunken brawls, as the English had introduced alcohol to the Indians. Louis Herbert and his family survived and had taken in a little boy from Madagascar, Africa, who had been abandoned by the English. When Champlain returned, there were English ships in the St. Lawrence, but they left without a fight. They were loaded with a cargo of fish and furs and were anxious to return home.

Everyone was put to work rebuilding. Another task that Champlain began immediately was securing the support of his former Indian allies. He convinced them not to trade with the English down river and reminded them of all the help the French had given them against the Iroquois. The local Montagnais chief promised loyalty to the point of "even cultivating grain," something the local Indians had resisted until now. Champlain predicted, "Our sons shall wed your daughters and henceforth we shall be one people." This was to prove true later on, with French-Indian intermarriage in Canada.

When he was about 63 years old, Champlain set up a new fortified trading post north of Quebec to protect the French from Iroquois raids. In 1633 he requested more soldiers from the King, but it was not granted for 31 years. In 1664 the King took direct control of Canada, but it was too late for the Hurons, who were conquered by the Iroquois in 1649.

In spite of a constant threat of Iroquois attack, during Champlain's last years, fur trade prospered. The Hundred Associates Company provided Quebec with enough supplies to get through the winter and spring each year. The fall of 1635 was Champlain's last; in October he suffered a paralytic stroke and never left his bed again. He died on Christmas Day 1635. Before leaving Helene in France in 1633, Champlain had put his affairs in order and made sure his wife would inherit his property. Helene joined a convent in France after her husband's death. Interestingly, Champlain's will provided money to Abraham Martin for clearing land in Quebec that later became known as the Plains of

Abraham. This would be the site of the decisive battle fought in 1759.

In spite of his bravery, dedication, and honor as a leader, in his lifetime Champlain never received recognition as "the Father of New France." This title was given to him in the 1800s, long after his death. In a space of 32 years he had crossed the Atlantic 23 times. He had risked his life many times. He wrote four books filled with information, maps, sketches, and details about the geography and people in North America that inspired further exploration and settlement in the New World.

Chapter 9
Henry Hudson's Final Attempt to Find a Northwest Passage, 1609-1611

Since King James I of England had placed Hudson under house arrest when Hudson and his crew returned to England in the fall of 1609, the *Half Moon* was unable to return to Amsterdam until July. Meanwhile, three influential London merchants formed the Company of Gentlemen and persuaded the king that Hudson should command the large, heavy bark *Discovery* in 1610. At 65 feet long, it was the largest ship he had commanded. It carried a crew of 22. By now Hudson realized the Northwest Passage was not located along the eastern coast of North America as Captain John Smith's map had suggested. Instead he believed it would be found somewhere beyond the Davis Strait in Arctic Canada above 60 degrees north latitude.

What is known of Henry Hudson's fourth voyage comes

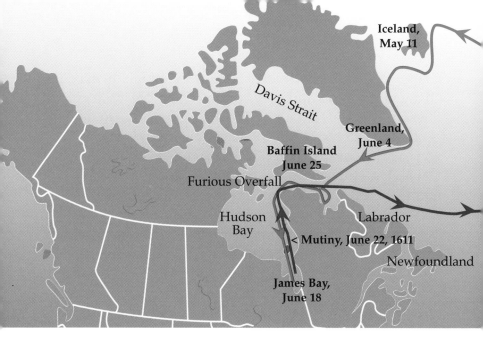

Hudson's last voyage aboard the *Discovery*, 1610-1611

from a small portion of his own journal which abruptly
ended August 1, 1610, and from a journal written by
Abacuk Prickett of events between April 17, 1610, and the
arrival of the *Discovery* in Plymouth, England the next year.

As captain, Hudson had the authority to pick his own
crew. His son John and his loyal carpenter, Philip Staffe,
remained with him. He hired Robert Juet again as first
mate, in spite of the trouble Juet had caused on previous
voyages. It may be that Hudson trusted Juet's navigational
skills and experience enough to overlook his character. The
Discovery raised anchor on April 17, 1610, and sailed down
the Thames River. Only five days into the voyage Hudson
fired a man named Coleburne, who had been hired by the
company, and replaced him with a family friend, young
Henry Greene. Mr. Greene proved to be troublesome, fighting with other crew members. When the ship reached Iceland, they saw an erupting volcano, which the superstitious
crew took as a bad omen. Before reaching Greenland, First
Mate Juet, after having a few drinks, accused Greene of
being Hudson's spy. Hudson became so angry at this

charge, he almost put Juet ashore in Iceland. However, he changed his mind and they continued on. Near Greenland the ship encountered a pod of whales but came to no harm. By June 25 the *Discovery* reached the Davis Strait, a waterway named for the 1587 voyage of explorer John Davis. The ship continued on to the Furious Overfall, so named because of the dangerous currents and whirlpools that frightened the crew. Once past this point they began to see larger and more numerous icebergs. At least once they had to anchor to avoid being blown into the icebergs.

Hudson sent Prickett, Green, and Bylot ashore to hunt wild game. They spotted partridges and a herd of grazing deer, but they were not successful in shooting any. They would have had to return empty-handed except they came upon some stone mounds. These were storehouses the Inuits had built to preserve game for the winter. Prickett recorded, "They were full of fowl (game birds) hung by their necks." The sailors helped themselves to the birds. They wanted to stay longer in hopes of further replenishing the ship's food supply, but Hudson was in a hurry to continue on before winter set in. He was convinced that once past the Furious Overfall the waters would widen into the legendary body of water called the Strait of Anian. Geographers of the 1600s believed this led to China.

In August the *Discovery* anchored in a narrow channel. Hudson sent three men to climb a cliff and report back what lay ahead. They excitedly described a large body of water as far as the eye could see. Hudson was thrilled; surely this was what he had been looking for, a sea leading to the Pacific Ocean. In reality they had just discovered the bay later named for Hudson, a cold, dangerous body of water that remains frozen for over half the year.

During the next three months Hudson charted the coastline of the eastern shore of Hudson Bay. Meanwhile the crew was becoming increasingly restless, nervous, and eager to leave. The northern winter was fast approaching, and their food supplies were getting low. First Mate Juet was again openly critical of Hudson. A little too late, Hudson tried to show his authority and put Juet on trial. The crew was sworn to tell the truth. Some testified that Juet had encouraged the men to keep their loaded muskets and swords ready to mutiny. The crew now sided with their captain. Hudson took Juet's position away, making Robert Bylot the new first mate, and he cut Juet's wages.

The trial did not solve the day-to-day problems of weather and poor conditions, however. Ice, fog, and freezing rain made working on deck hazardous. After a week of severe storms, Hudson ordered the ship to sail on, in spite of the conditions. The crew objected that it was too dangerous. One man had already died while working on deck. The ship's carpenter cautioned Hudson about getting too close to the rocks. Sure enough, one night the ship ran aground on the rocks, but luckily no major damage was done. It was becoming clear to the crew that Hudson seemed obsessed with reaching the Pacific, and he seemed to show little concern about endangering his men.

By the end of October it also became clear that the *Discovery* would be trapped for the winter in James Bay, the southern extension of Hudson Bay. Hudson sent a party out to find a suitable spot to spend the winter. The crew hauled the ship onto the shore. They had barely enough food to last the six months. The men went out to hunt for game and shot birds. In December Hudson ordered the ship's carpenter, Philip Staffe, to build a shelter, even threatening to shoot him if he refused. But Hudson had waited too long; the wood and nails were frozen too hard to use.

The suffering over the winter was terrible. Many became ill with scurvy, and one man, John Williams, died. Aboard ship it was the custom when a sailor died, to auction off his belongings so the money could be sent to his family. Hudson used poor judgment by allowing Henry Greene to claim Williams' coat for himself. This caused hard feelings among the crew. Later, when Hudson became annoyed with Greene for his disobedience, he took the coat away and gave it to Robert Bylot. Then Greene turned against Hudson. He would play an important part in the mutiny that was brewing.

At first the men were able to shoot enough birds to keep from starving, but gradually as winter wore on, the birds disappeared. The starving crew had to forage for anything they could possibly eat, even moss and frogs. Dr. Wilson, the ship's surgeon, made a tea from some sticky buds they found, and used it to treat scurvy and other sicknesses. The crew saw very few Inuits. Only one came to trade, and he brought animal pelts, not food. They tried to make him understand they would trade for food, but he never returned.

When the ice began to break up, several sailors were able to net 500 fish. Prickett's journal states: "[They] were as big as good herring, and [we got] some trout, which gave us all some hope of supplying our meals." Later they caught 80 small fish, "a poor relief for so many hungry bellies." The men were suspicious that Hudson was hoarding food himself, so Hudson ordered the bread chests opened and divided up all the remaining bread. He did the same with their supply of cheese. Some of the men ate their entire share immediately, running out of food. Hudson then committed another mistake in judgment. He ordered the crew's sea chests opened to search for hoarded food. A sailor's sea chest was his only private thing on the ship, and the men were furious.

Three days later the mutiny that had been simmering for almost the entire voyage broke out. Led by Juet and the treacherous Henry Greene, a group of men seized and bound Hudson. In his journal Abacuk Prickett claimed he did not support the mutineers and tried to talk them out of it. Hudson's journal did not survive to confirm this, so history only has Prickett's own word for it. Prickett reminded the mutineers they'd be hung for mutiny if they ever returned to England, and they'd never see their families again. The desperate men told him they would rather take a chance at being "hung at home than starved abroad."

Hudson and others being set adrift after the mutiny.
(Drawing by Andrew Thompson)

Hudson, his son John, Philip Staffe, who remained loyal, and six other men, most of whom were sick, were placed in a small rowboat and set adrift in Hudson Bay. None of them were ever seen or heard from again, and it is presumed they all perished.

Henry Greene took command of the *Discovery*, but it did not go well. He ordered the ship searched for food, still suspecting hoarding, but no more food was found. While attempting to get food from the Inuits, the crew was attacked. Greene and three others died of their wounds. Only nine men had survived thus far, and then Juet died of starvation. The eight remaining men somehow made it to the coast of Ireland and eventually to London.

They told their tale of the doomed voyage, blaming the mutiny on Juet and Greene, both conveniently dead, and on Hudson's failure as a captain. It took five years to bring them to trial, and they were never punished. This may have been because they were the only living people who knew what Hudson had discovered and would be able to direct future exploration.

Several years later, ships were sent out again to Hudson Bay to seek the Northwest Passage and find any signs of survivors from Hudson's little group. Neither goal was achieved. The western limit of Hudson Bay was discovered, and ice blocked further passage, ending the hope this was the gateway to the Pacific. No survivors were found, although years later fur trappers for the Hudson Bay Company claimed to have seen ruins of a crude house, possibly built by Philip Staffe. There were also stories about a band of white men who joined a native tribe, but that was never proved.

Three years after Hudson's presumed death, his widow Katherine applied to the East India Company on behalf of her youngest son, Richard. They gave him a place on a ship, and he later had a high position with the company. Mrs. Hudson was intelligent and persuasive, and she got a job with the East India Company as well, handling the indigo trade with India.

Chapter 10
The Legacy of Champlain and Hudson

Samuel de Champlain and Henry Hudson each made important contributions to history. Both explored modern-day New York State in 1609. Their explorations were separated by a few months and less than 100 miles. They both might have claimed territory in the New World for France, had the Dutch not beaten King Henry IV in giving Hudson a contract to explore.

Both men were skilled navigators and mapmakers, who charted previously unknown waters. They were men of courage and incredible determination, enduring many hardships and dangers to seek a northern water passage to Asia. Thanks to their perseverance, much was learned about North American geography, climate, animal and plant life, and the native peoples they encountered.

The French culture and language introduced by Champlain remains alive and well today in the Canadian provinces of Quebec and New Brunswick. Canada is bilingual, with both French and English spoken there long after the end of the French and Indian War in 1763. Many French place names still exist since Champlain's time: St. Croix, Port Royal, Quebec, Montreal, Richelieu River, Lake Champlain, Isle au Haut, to name a few.

The Dutch influence in present-day New York State may not seem as obvious. Dutch is no longer commonly spoken. The settlement of New Amsterdam was started as a result of Henry Hudson's explorations. New Amsterdam, now one of the wealthiest and largest commercial centers of the world, New York City, still reflects the "melting pot" atmosphere it had when it was Dutch. The colony from its start welcomed people of all countries and religions. Many different languages were spoken there, which remains true today. Many places named by the Dutch still exist around Manhattan and the Hudson River Valley, such as Harlem, Brooklyn, Wall Street, the Bowery, Peekskill, Catskill, Amsterdam, Greenbush, and Rotterdam. Dutch children were the first to hang up stockings for St. Nicholas, or Santa Claus, to fill, a custom that seems typically American today.

One of the most important areas of influence by Champlain and Hudson was on the culture and lives of the Indians. Before these explorers came, the Indians had fought over control of territory, primarily for hunting grounds and land for growing crops of corn, beans, and squash. With the arrival of the Europeans, another area of dispute arose: control of the profitable fur trade. The French, with their superior weapon, the arquebus, helped their Huron allies win two battles against the Mohawk Iroquois. In the end, however, the long ongoing warfare between them led to the near-extinction of the Huron, who eventually lost. Champlain's attack on the Onondaga Iroquois in central New York State, as well as later French attacks, caused the Iroquois to side with the British in the French and Indian War. This in turn brought about the loss of French control of Canada.

Hudson traded with Indians along his exploration routes, but he did little to establish friendly relations with them. The trade goods both he and Champlain brought also changed the Indian culture from its use of traditional items like stone axes and clay pots, to iron goods, such as knives, hatchets, and cooking pots, and European blankets and shirts. The Indians were quick to recognize the advantages of firearms, and desired to replace their traditional bows and arrows with guns, not only for defense, but also for hunting.

Perhaps the most negative effect of European contact with the Indians was the spread of contagious diseases. The Indians, who had no natural immunity, died by the thousands from diseases such as measles and smallpox brought over by the Europeans. It is interesting to note that the Indians gave the explorers some of their natural remedies, such as white cedar bark tea to cure scurvy.

The most important legacy left by Champlain and Hudson might be considered accidental. In their persistent, but failed, attempts to find a water passage to Asia, they explored vast areas of unknown territory filled with extensive forests, natural resources, inlets and bays suitable for harbors and settlements, and waters filled with fish. The desire by European nations to claim these resources and territory, encouraged later exploration and settlement. They did not find a Northwest Passage; it would not happen until almost 300 years later, when the Norwegian explorer Amundsen managed to navigate a northern route. It took him two years. If global warming continues to shrink the Arctic ice, some day it may be possible to sail northwest from Europe to Asia, just as Hudson and Champlain dreamed.

Epilogue:
Celebrations Past and Future

The year 1909 marked the 300th anniversary of Samuel de Champlain's discovery of Lake Champlain and Henry Hudson's voyage up the Hudson River. Celebrations were held along these waterways, and replicas of the *Don de Dieu* and the *Half Moon* were built.

The Samuel de Champlain Tercentennial Celebration took place from July 4 to July 9, 1909, throughout the Champlain Valley. The celebration was planned jointly by New York and Vermont. Events were scheduled in succession, beginning in Crown Point and continuing on to Ticonderoga, Burlington, Plattsburgh, and ending on July 9 on Isle La Motte, Vermont. The two states jointly erected a monument at Crown Point to commemorate the anniversary.

The events included speeches by the governors of New York and Vermont and U.S. President William Taft. There were parades with military units and bands. Mock battles were staged at Crown Point and Ticonderoga. A Canadian, who had been in charge of Canada's 300th anniversary of the founding of Quebec the previous year, organized Indian pageants. Thousands of people all along Lake Champlain attended the celebrations.

The Tercentennial for Henry Hudson's 1609 voyage up the Hudson River was held from September 25 to October 9, 1909, the time of year in which he actually had explored the Hudson River. It was celebrated jointly with the 100th anniversary of Robert Fulton's invention of the steamboat. The Dutch government gave the United States a replica of the *Half Moon* for the occasion. It was brought to the United States as deck cargo aboard a Holland America Line steamship. This shows how small Hudson's ship was compared to modern ocean liners.

Throughout the last week of September 1909, many events were held around New York City. Large parades, some five miles long, included elaborate floats, units from all branches of the U.S. military, foreign military units, and groups of Civil War veterans. Wilbur Wright was paid $15,000 to demonstrate his plane, *Flyer*, to the public for the first time.

The replica of the *Half Moon* was destroyed by a fire in 1934. In 1989 a new replica was built in Albany, New York. It has since sailed up and down the Hudson River as a traveling historical and educational exhibit.

As the 400th anniversary of Champlain's and Hudson's explorations approaches in 2009, it is likely many events will be scheduled in the United States and Canada. With the invention of television and satellite communication that was not available in 1909, more people than ever before will be able to see the events and celebrate the achievements of these two remarkable explorers.

The Champlain Monument at Crown Point, New York.

Champlain and Hudson
Timeline

1453 Fall of Constantinople to Turks, blocking overland trade with Asia

1494 The Pope divides the known world between Spain and Portugal

1524 Giovanni da Verrazano discovers the Hudson River while exploring for France

1570? Samuel de Champlain is born in Brouage, France Henry Hudson is born in Hoddersdon, England (? = exact dates unknown)

1587 Legend about Hudson sailing with John Davis to seek a northwest passage

1594 Champlain serves as soldier to help France defeat Spain

1599-1601 Champlain sails to Spanish West Indies, later publishes a journal

1603 Champlain sails up the St. Lawrence to Montreal

1604 Champlain helps establish fur trade center at Sainte Croix, Canada

1604-1606 Champlain makes three exploratory journeys down the New England coast

1605-1607 Champlain established Order of Good Cheer at Port Royal Habitation

1607 Hudson attempts to find a northeast passage to Asia over the North Pole

1608 Hudson tries again to find a northeast passage to Asia

1608 Champlain helps build the Quebec Habitation

July 1609 Champlain helps defeat the Mohawk Iroquois at Lake Champlain

Sept. 1609 Hudson sails the *Half Moon* up the Hudson River as far as Albany

April 1610 Hudson sails the *Discovery* to find the Northwest Passage

June 1610	Champlain's second battle with the Mohawk Iroquois
Dec. 1610	Champlain marries Helene Boulle in Paris
Nov. 1-Jun.18, 1611	Hudson and crew winter in James Bay
Jun. 1611	Mutiny aboard the *Discovery*, Hudson and others set adrift to die
Oct. 1611	Eight surviving mutineers arrive in England and are imprisoned
1613	Champlain publishes book, *Les Voyages*, and sails up the Ottawa River
1615	Champlain travels up the Ottawa River again and on to Lake Huron
Oct. 1615	Champlain helps his Indian allies attack Onondaga Iroquois village
1615-1616	Champlain winters with the Huron
1617	Hudson's mutinous crew put on trial
1617	Former crew member Bylot sails the *Discovery* to search for a northwest passage
1620-1624	Champlain's wife Helene lives in New France
April 1627	Cardinal Richelieu organizes the Company of Canada to bring settlers to New France
July 1629	Champlain surrenders Quebec to the English
1632	Treaty of St. Germain returns Quebec to the French
Mar. 1633	Champlain makes his last voyage to New France
Dec. 25, 1635	Champlain dies in Quebec
May 1626	Dutch governor Peter Minuit buys Manhattan Island from Indians for $24
Sept. 1664	The English take over New Netherlands from the Dutch
1763	The French and Indian War ends with France surrendering New France to England

Glossary

Note: words that are explained in the text are not included here.

archipelago	A chain of islands
arquebus	A gun used during Champlain's time. It was fired using black powder and a slow-burning match cord, also called a *mousquit* by the French
assassination	The killing of a ruler or important leader, usually for political reasons
astrolabe	A navigational tool used to measure a ship's latitude to determine location
barter	An exchange of goods; trade
calculated risk	A decision made after considering possible positive and negative outcomes
caulking	Material for sealing between the boards of a ship. A fiber called oakum was used.
charter	An official document stating the rights and duties of the group to which it was given.
city states	Independent territories that developed around a city
contagious disease	An illness that is easily spread from one person to another
dowry	A sum of money given to a husband by his wife's family when they married
dysentery	An intestinal illness often caused by bad food or unclean water
fathom	Nautical measurement of depth, equal to six feet
flotilla	A fleet of ships
forage	To hunt for wild foods
foremast	The forward mast of a ship
guilders	Dutch unit of money
hardtack	A type of hard, dry biscuit used aboard ship because it kept well without spoiling
hatter	Skilled workers in Europe who used beaver fur to make felt hats
hoard	To keep for one's own use
house arrest	Imprisonment within one's own house
ice floes	Masses of ice formed on the surface of a body of water

Indian wheat	Indian corn or maize grown by the Indians and traded to the Europeans
indigo	A dark blue vegetable dye
lead line	A rope used to measure water depth on a sailing ship. It had a lead weight on the end and was marked every fathom (six feet).
livre	French unit of money during Champlain's time
moat	A water-filled trench around a fort or castle, used for defense
monopoly	The exclusive right granted by the king to trade or sell goods in a certain area
mouth (of a river)	The place where a river empties into a sea or larger body of water
mutiny	A rebellion by the crew against the ship's captain
Polar projection	Maps that show the North or South Pole
portage	To travel on land, carrying one's canoe around obstacles such as rapids or waterfalls
quarterdeck	The upper deck of a ship, located toward the rear or stern of the ship
royal pension	A yearly sum of money given by the king
rules of warfare	A set of unwritten but accepted tactics enemy forces used against each other
scurvy	A disease caused by lack of vitamin C in the diet
sea chest	A chest or box that held a sailor's personal belongings
siege warfare	Style of warfare in which attackers surround a fort to force their way in, often using platforms to attack and get over the walls
source (of a river)	The place where a river begins
strait	A narrow waterway that connects two larger bodies of water
thunder tubes	The name North American Indians gave to the European guns
traitor	One who betrays or turns against his country or friends
treachery	Betrayal of trust, disloyalty
wampum	Strings of small shell beads set in patterns by the Indians for decoration or to mark events or ceremonies

Bibliography
Samuel de Champlain

(* Denotes a book for young readers)

Bishop, Morris. Champlain, *The Life of Fortitude.* London: Macdonald and Co. Ltd., 1949.

Buckell, Betty Ahearn. *Boldly into the Wilderness, Travelers in Upstate New York 1010-1646.* Queensbury NY: Buckle Press, 1999.

Calvert, Mary R. *Dawn over the Kennebec.* .Monmouth ME: Monmouth Press, 1983.

Cline, Duane A. *Navigation in the Age of Discovery.* Rogers AR: Montfleury Press, Inc., 1990.

Coulter, Tony. *Jacques Cartier and Samuel de Champlain, Exploration of Canada.* New York: Chelsea House Publishing, 1993. *

Dix, Edwin Asa. *Champlain the Founder of New France.* New York: D. Appleton and Company, 1903.

Hill, Henry Wayland. Secretary of the Commission. *The Champlain Tercentenary, First Report.* State of New York, 1913.

Jones, Elizabeth. *Gentlemen and Jesuits, Glory and Adventure in the Early Days of Acadia.* Halifax: Nimbus Publishing LTD, 2002.

Kaiser, James. *Acadia: The Complete Guide.* Singapore: Destination Press, 2005.

Livesey, Robert and A.G. Smith. *New France* (Discovering Canada series). Toronto: Stoddart Publishing Co. Ltd., 1990.

Moore, Christopher. *Champlain.* Toronto: Tundra Books, 2004.

Morganelli, Adrianna. *Samuel de Champlain, From New France to Cape Cod.* New York: Crabtree Publishing Company, 2006. *

Morison, Samuel Eliot. *Samuel de Champlain: Father of New France.* Boston: Little and Brown, 1972. *

Sonneborn, Liz. *Samuel de Champlain.* Danbury: Franklin Watts, 2001.*

Tercentenary Celebration of the Discovery of Lake Champlain and Vermont. Lake Champlain Tercentenary Committee of Vermont, 1910.

Bibliography
Henry Hudson

(* Denotes a book for young readers)

Diamant, Lincoln. *Hoopla on the Hudson, An Intimate View of New York's Great 1909 Hudson Fulton Celebration*. Fleischmanns NY: Purple Mountain Press, 2003.

Doak, Robin S. *Henry Hudson Searches for a Passage to Asia*. Minneapolis: Compass Point books, 2003 *

Gleason, Carrie. *Henry Hudson, Seeking the Northwest Passage*. New York: Crabtree Publishing Company, 2005. *

Goodman, Joan Elizabeth. *Beyond the Sea of Ice*. New York: Mikaya Press, 1999. *

Hamilton, Milton W. *Henry Hudson and the Dutch in New York*. Albany: The University of the State of New York, 1964.

Harley, Ruth. *Henry Hudson*. Mahwah NJ: Troll Associates, 1979. *

Janvier, Thomas A. *Henry Hudson, A Brief Statement of his Aims and hisAchievements*. New York: Harper and Bros., 1909.

Johnson, Donald S. *Charting the Sea of Darkness*. Kodansha America, Inc., 1995.

Juet, Robert. *Juet's Journal, the Voyage of the Half Moon from 4 April to 7 November 1609*. Ed. Robert M. Lunny. Newark NJ: New Jersey Historical Society, 1959.

Powys, Llewelyn. *Henry Hudson*. New York: Harper and Brothers, 1928.

Santella, Andrew. *Henry Hudson*. Danbury: Franklin Watts, 2001. *

Vail, Phillip. *The Magnificent Adventures of Henry Hudson*. New York: Dodd, Mead, and Co., 1965.

Weiner, Eric. *Henry Hudson, Master Explorer*. New York: Dell, 1991*

West, Tracey. *Voyage of the Half Moon*. New York: Silver Moon Press, 1993. *

Index

Acadia, 11,14, 56
Agnonha, (Iron People), 54
Albany, 49, 62
Alcohol, 64
Algonquin, 10, 31, 32, 34
Amsterdam, 37, 66, 74
Amundsen, 75
Aptuxet Indians, 16
Arctic, 39
    ice, 75
    summer, 24, 25
Arquebus, 27, 28 (picture), 31, 34, 52,
    57, 58, 59, 74
Arranged marriage, 53
Arrow, broken, 48
    wound (Champlain), 52, 59
Asia, 7,11,12,19, 20, 21, 23, 24, 26, 36,
    44, 51, 52, 61
Astrolabe, 56

Barter, 18, 40, 45, 46, 47
Basques, 29, 62
Bay of Fundy, 13, 14
Beaver skins, 35 (ill.), 42, 54, 63
Beef, pickled, 22, 38
Bilingual, 73
Boston Bay, 16
Boulle, Helene, 53, 62, 63, 65
Bowery, 74
Brewerton, 57
Brooklyn, 74
Brouage, 7
Brule, Etienne, 31, 56, 57, 59, 63
Burlington, 75
Bylot, Robert, 69, 70

Caboto, Giovanni, 7
Cahiague, 57
Cannon, 50
Canoes, birchbark, 33 (ill.), 34, 41, 46,
    47, 54
Cape Cod, 16, 18, 43
Cartier, Jacques, 10,15, 57
Catskill, 74
    mountains, 47

Champlain Valley, 75
Chatham, 18
Charity, 63
China, 11,12, 68
Christmas Day (1635), 65
Codfish, 7, 41, 43
    salted, 43
Coleburne, 67
Colman, John, 22, 38, 44, 45
Colman's Point, 45
Columbus, Christopher, 12
Company of Gentlemen, 66
Copper deposits, 14
    kettles, 42
Corn hills, 15
Crown Point, 75

da Gama, Vasco, 11
Dartmouth, 51
Davis, John, 12, 68
Davis Strait, 26, 39, 66, 68
Delaware Bay, 43
de Monts, Sieur, 11,13, 15, 16, 18, 29
Desportes, Pierre, 62
Discovery, 66, 67, 68, 69, 72
Diseases, 74
Dog meat, 47, 59
Don de Dieu, Le, 27 (ill.), 29, 75
Dowry, 53
Dream, (Champlain's), 32
Dutch, competition, 62
    influence, 50, 51, 73
    sailors, 38, 39, 44
    settlement, 29, 51, 61, 73
Dutch East India Company, 12, 26, 36,
    37, 38
Duval, Jean, 30

East India Company, 72
East Indies, 39, 64
Eels, smoked, 30

Faeroe Islands, 40
Faith, 63
Father of New France, 61, 64, 66

Fathom, 22, 46
Fort Crozat, 8
Fort Orange, 56
French, culture, 73
    fishing fleets, 40
    fur traders, 41, 54
French and Indian War, 73, 74
Frobisher, Martin, 9
Fulton, Robert, 76
Furious Overfall, 39, 68
Fur trade, 29, 34, 35, 50, 53, 54, 59,
    61, 64, 65, 74

Garfish, monster, 35
Genoa, 7
Georgian Bay, 57
Gig, 49, 50
Global warming, 75
Gold, 9, 14, 41, 42
Governor of New France, 54, 64
Grand Banks, 7, 35, 40
Grant's Tomb, 46
Grapes, wild, 43
Great Ice Barrier, 24
Great Lakes, 38
Great Salt Sea, 52, 54
Greenbush, 74
Greene, Henry, 67, 68, 70, 72
Greenland, 22, 67-68

Hague, (The), 36
Hakluyt, Richard, 20
Half Moon, The, 38, 40 , 43, 44, 45, 46,
    47, 49, 50, 66, 75
    replica, 76
Hardtack biscuits, 41
Harlem, 74
Haudenosaunee Confederacy, 6
Hellaine, Guillaume, 9
Hemlock bedding, 59
Henderson Harbor, 57
Herbert, Louis, 61, 62, 64
Herring
    fresh, 41
    salted, 38
Hoarding (food), 70, 72
Hoboken, 50
Hoddersdon, 11

Holland, 26, 27, 36, 50, 51
Honfleur, 10
Hope, 63
Hopewell, The, 13, 20, 22, 23 (map),
    24, 26
Hostages, 45, 47, 50
House arrest, 51
Hudson Bay, 54, 55, 56, 67 (map), 68,
    69, 71-72
Hudson Bay Company, 72
Hudson, John, 13, 21, 22, 38, 54, 67, 71
Hudson, Katherine, 13, 21, 72
Hudson, Richard, 13, 72
Hudson River, 6, 44, 46, 49, 75, 78
Huguenots, 8
Hundred Associates, The, 64-65
Huron Indians, 31, 34, 52, 56, 59, 57,
    58, 65, 74
Huronia, 57, 59

Icebergs, 24, 68
Ice floes, 14
Iceland, 51, 67
India, 11, 72
Indian wheat, 44
Indigo, 72
Intermarriage, 65
Inuit, 70
    attack, 72
    storehouses, 68
Ireland, 72
Iron, cooking pots, 54, 74
    hatchets, 74
Iroquois, 6, 10, 27, 31, 32, 34, 52, 59,
    61
    raids, 65
Isle La Motte, 75

James Bay, 69
Jamestown, 38, 43
Journals, Henry Hudson, 25, 26, 46,
    48, 67, 71
    Robert Juet, 38, 39, 42, 43, 44, 45,
    46
    Abacuk Prickett, 67, 68, 70, 71
Juet, Robert, 26, 38, 44, 48, 50, 67-69,
    70, 72

Kebec (Quebec), 10, 30
King Henry IV, 37, 52, 73
King James, 26, 51, 66
King Louis XIII, 52, 63
Knives, stone, 41

Labrador, 39
La Chine Rapids, 54, 56, 60
Lake Champlain battle of 1609, 32-34
Lake Huron, 57
Lake St. Louis (Ontario), 57
Land grant, 13
Lenape Indians, 44
Livres, 8
Lobsters, 42
Loincloth, 41

Maine, 11, 13, 15, 18, 43
Madagascar, 65
Manhattan Island, 44, 51
Mannahatas, 44
Mapmakers, 8, 21, 73
Marsolet, Nicolas, 31
Martin, Abraham, 65
Masts, 38, 42
Measles, 74
Medici, Marie de, 52
Melting pot, 73
Mermaids, 25
Mirrors, 41, 42, 46
Micmac Indians, 30
Moccasins, 41
Mohawk Indians, 6, 27, 32, 33, 34, 35,
    52, 62, 74
Mohican Indians, 47, 62
Montagnais Indians, 10, 30, 31, 52, 62,
    63, 65
Montreal, 54, 55, 56
Mount Mansfield, 32
Mud banks, 50
Muhheakunnuck, 46
Mullet, 44
Muscovy Company, 11,13, 21, 24, 26,
    36
Mutiny, 26, 30, 39, 70-71

Nauset Indians, 16
Navigational skills, 5, 8, 73

Neptune play, 18
New Amsterdam, 73
New Brunswick, 11,13, 73
Newfoundland, 35, 40
New France, 13, 55, 56, 60, 61, 64, 66
New Holland, 43
New Netherlands, 50
New York City, 51, 73
Northeast Passage, 23, 24, 36, 37
North Pole, 20, 21, 24
    route, 20
Northwest Passage, 10, 12, 29, 37, 51,
    60, 66, 72, 75
Norumbega, 14
Nova Scotia, 11, 13, 16
Nova Zembla, 21, 23 (map), 24, 25
Norwegian Current, 24

Oak bark, 48
Ob River, 21
Ocean tides, 46
Oneida Lake, 57
Onondaga Indians, 57, 58, 59, 74
Onondaga village, 57-58 (ill.)
Order of Good Cheer, 18
Orillia, 57
Oswego County, 57
Ottawa, 56, 57
Ottawa River, 54, 55, 57
Outaouais Indians, 57
Outlet (of Lake Champlain), 34
Oysters, 46

Pacific Ocean, 38, 39, 43, 68, 69
Pageant (Indian), 76
Palisades, 46
Palm trees, 33
Paralytic stroke, 65
Peekskill, 46, 50
Penobscot Algonquins, 41
Penobscot Bay, 14, 16, 41, 43
Pension, royal, 10
Pigeon, roasted, 47
Pilgrims, 16
Plains of Abraham, 65
Plancius, Peter, 36
Plattsburgh, 75
Plums, wild, 44

Plymouth, England, 63, 67
Plymouth Harbor, 16
Poison ivy, 44
Polar Projection Map, 20
Portage, 55-56
Port Royal, 16, 17 (ill.,map), 18, 19, 56
Port St. Louis, 17 (map)
Prickett, Abacuk, 67, 68, 71
Protestants, 64
Pulaski, 57
Pumpkins, 47

Quadricentennial Anniversary, 76
Quarterdeck, 39, 46
Quartermaster, 8
Quebec, 19, 29, 30, 31, 34, 52, 61, 62,
    63, 64, 73
    surrender of, 63

Red gowns, 42
Renaissance, 7
Revenge, (Mohawk), 52
Richelieu, Cardinal, 64
Richelieu River, 31
River of Mountains, 27, 46
Rotterdam, 74

Saint Nicholas, 74
Sainte-Croix, 13, 14 (ill.), 15
Salmon River, 57
Salt, 7, 22
Schenectadea, 49
Scurvy, 15, 18, 30, 69, 70, 75
Seasickness, 39
Seigneurial system, 64
Siege warfare, 58
Slake, 39
Smallpox, 74
Smeerenburg, 22
Smith, Captain John, 39, 43, 66
Souvenirs, 35
Spice Islands, 11, 12
Spice trade, 5, 7, 11, 12
Spitsbergen, 22, 23 (map), 24, 26, 38
Staffe, Philip, 67, 69, 71

Staten Island, 44
St. Ethelburga, 22
St. Lawrence River, 29, 30, 61, 62, 65
Strait of Anian, 68
Sturgeon, 18
Supply ships, annual, 9, 30, 61
Susquehannock Indians, 57, 59

Tadoussac, 10, 29, 53
Taft, President William, 76
Tappan Zee, 46
Tercentennial Anniversary, 75-76
Thames River, 67
Thorne, Robert, 20
Ticonderoga, 75
Tobacco, green, 44
Torture, 32, 57
Trade monopoly, 13, 18, 30, 54
Trout, 70

Venice, 7
Venison, 18, 49
Verrazano. Giovanni da, 7, 44, 45
Vignau, Nicolas, 54
Virginia, 38
Volcano, 67
Voyages, Les, 14 (ill.), 17 (ill.), 53 (ill.),
    54

Walrus, 24, 25 (ill.)
Wall Street, 74
Wampum, 49
War party, 57, 59
Waterford, 49
West Indies, 10, 33, 64
West Point, 47
Whales, 22
    oil, 22
    pod, 68
Whirlpool, 55
White cedar bark, 15 (ill.) 75
Williams, John, 69
Wilson, Dr., 70
Wright, Wilbur, 76

"Don Thompson has been portraying the life of Henry Hudson for my fourth graders for many years. He has a wealth of knowledge and the children are always eager to participate in his hands-on, engaging presentation. It feels as if we jump back in time! It is always one of the highlights of the year when 'Henry Hudson' comes to visit the classroom. History becomes 'real' for my pupils."

—Faith Halnon, Granville Elemtary School, Granville, NY

"During a social studies class, third and fourth grade students at Holy Cross School had a visit from the famous explorers Samuel de Champlain and Henry Hudson (Don Thompson). The explorers brought copies of the maps used on their voyages and shared many artifact replicas, which the students were invited to touch and examine. The students were also taught how the ships' crews met the many challenges of their voyages."

—Judith Bierman, Holy Cross School, Dewitt, New York

DONALD THOMPSON makes presentations as Champlain and Hudson for schools, libraries, historical societies, and senior groups. To book, call Don in Vermont at 802-468-5309 (May through November) or in Florida at 941-776-1714 (December through April).

PURPLE MOUNTAIN PRESS publishes books about New York State and colonial and maritime history. Other books for young readers include *The Mohicans* and *Sybil Ludington*. For a free catalog, call 1-800-325-2665 or email purple@catskill.net; on the web at www.catskill.net/purple.